The Amazing Life of Johnny Saint Gold

By Robert Santoro

Dedicated to my wife Barbara and my son James.

Without your support, this book would not be possible.

Chapter One

The Boy from Avellino

Johnny opened his eyes and he felt like it was going to be a good day. He lived with his older brother Anthony. Though he was older, Anthony was only fourteen-years-old. Together with his five-year-old sister Theresa, and his parents Dominic and Phyllis, they lived in a small farmhouse on the Avellino hillside in Italy. Johnny was nine-years-old and worked hard on the family farm. For his birthday his father gave him his own young colt he named Bella. It was an immediate bond as Johnny and Bella were inseparable.

As was the custom of the day, the family farm was passed on to the male gender for as long as anyone could remember. It was expected that it would be passed on to Anthony and Johnny when Dominic and Phyllis had passed away. Theresa was expected to marry and hopefully provided for by her future husband. If she did not marry, it was expected that Anthony and Johnny would provide for her. It was the late eighteen-hundreds and generations-long traditions still defined the culture.

The two boys spent most of their daytime hours tending to the farm work. Only when there was time available, the boys were home-schooled by their mother Phyllis. She insisted that they should be able to read fluently and have a good understanding of math. She believed this younger generation would be challenged for physical stamina, but also, they must have the ability to use their minds, and to understand that there is more to life than just farming.

Dominic did not agree. He spent his whole life working on the farm and felt the boys should not be exposed to any other non-farming occupational activities. After all, he had taught his boys how to fix roofs, how to build stone walls, and how to hunt. This was all in addition to running the farm. He taught them all they needed to know to survive and care for their family, as did he and his father. To appease Phyllis, he let her home school them as long as the boys did not neglect their farm duties.

Dominic had to admit to himself that the boys seemed smarter and more mature than he was at their age. In his mind he took most of the credit for the boy's progress. His mother's schooling may have also helped, but he would never mention it or give her any credit.

It was Saturday and it was Johnny's day to watch over and guard the community food storage barn. This was located on his father's farm. A group of the local farms had formed a cooperative to store the fruits of their harvest. His farm was one of the largest in the cooperative and the barn was centrally located to the other farm members. Each day, a local youngster stood at watch to alert the farmers if any transients happened to come by to try to steal some of the cooperatives' food storage. There was a big bell that would warn the farmers if there was a problem.

Johnny rang the alert bell once in the past when he was working in the small garden just outside the barn. He did this when two travelers had approached him after coming off the dirt road that ran adjacent to the barn. The road was far enough away that whoever was on guard had time to signal for help. Within minutes several of the farmers on horseback had arrived to check out who the two visitors were. As it was, the two visitors were only looking for directions to another farm.

Johnny was embarrassed that he had sounded the alarm. He thought he should have challenged them alone without ringing the bell. He was tall for his age and sometimes wanted to pretend he was older, but there were two of them. He made the decision to call for help. When he returned home that evening, his father complemented him for sounding the alarm. Better to be safe than sorry. His father thought Johnny was extremely intelligent for as young as he was and trusted his judgment. Dominic loved all his children, but he knew that there was something very special about Johnny.

The next morning was uneventful. Johnny arrived at the barn at 8:00 AM to relieve the night guard. He worked the garden until noon and then took a break to sit under the shade of a tall tree. He closed his eyes and thought about the young girl he met at the harvest party. She had long black hair and was very pretty. He had known her for several years, but he recently noticed how friendly she had become. He really enjoyed being with her.

The sun was strong and sitting in the shade felt restful. Suddenly, he felt a very small vibration radiating from the ground. He jumped to his feet abruptly and looked around to see what was happening. The vibration grew stronger and a thumping noise appeared to be coming from the road. It was unlike anything he had ever heard.

Johnny ran toward the road and reached the wooden fence separating the farm and the dirt roadway. The fence consisted of vertical upright wooden posts buried securely in the ground at approximately eight-foot intervals with three wooden horizontal posts at each section connecting the upright posts. The top railing was approximately four feet high. Johnny would remember that fence for the rest of his life.

Johnny looked down the road and saw where the rumbling and noise was coming from. It looked like many mounted riders and wagons. The noise was incredible. The caravan was coming and would shortly pass right by where he was standing. To get a better look at this impressive parade, he climbed up two of the bottom fence railings. He leaned forward with his knees against the top railing and balanced himself with his left hand holding on to the vertical post, so he would not fall headfirst over the fence.

What a sight to behold! It was the Italian military passing by him. Johnny had never seen anything like it. He had heard about the Italian mounted military, but to see them so close was unimaginable. At first, many columns of mounted soldiers rode by. Looking further behind them, Johnny saw that there were many open wagons.

Most of his friends talked often about someday joining the military and traveling out of their province. However, no one that he knew ever left the province. They were born there, and they died there.

A mounted soldier rode over to Johnny and bent over to reach out to shake Johnny's right hand. He appeared huge and handsome in his uniform with many stripes on his sleeves. The soldier road a beautiful black steed and galloped alongside, but he was not part of the main column. Johnny reached out to shake the soldier's hand. He was so excited and thought what a tribute this was. He would tell all his friends, his father and brother how exciting it was to shake the soldier's hand. Johnny thought, "I will never forget this."

He was correct. He would never forget this event which led to an incredible journey and new start in life for young Johnny.

Chapter Two
From Captive to Soldier

Their hands touched but the mounted soldier reached out and he let his hand slide down to Johnny's elbow. This was not what Johnny had expected. The soldier then closed his hand tightly around Johnny's forearm. He pulled up straight and lifted him over the fence dragging him to the rear of one of the open carts that had stopped in the center of the road. Two soldiers jumped out to assist in throwing him into the cart. Things were happening too fast. Johnny tried to resist but was quickly overwhelmed by the two soldiers.

They held him face down in the cart. When he tried to resist, one sat on him and the other pushed the butt of his rifle down hard on Johnny's back. The pain was

The Italian Militia – Late Eighteen-Hundreds

terrible, and he almost blacked out. They said if he continued to resist, they would tie his hands and feet. The wagon had stopped long enough to grab him and then proceeded with their captive. Johnny was told there was no chance to escape and if he was able to jump out of the cart before they reached their destination, they would shoot him as a deserter.

The right side of Johnny's face was forced flat on to the floor of the cart by the pressure of the rifle butt pushed into his back and he could only look to his left. There were other young occupants sitting down on the seat of that side of the cart. He assumed that there were more sitting on the other side, out of his view. Johnny thought the other children had met the same fate as he had. One of the younger captives was crying softly.

One of the soldiers told Johnny that he was now property of the Italian militia. Since there was a shortage of young adult men, younger male recruits, most of them children, were needed to help and work as stable hands and perform other non-combative supportive jobs in the military. The soldier told him he should be proud to serve his country at such a young age and he would be eventually discharged, and able to be returned home sometime in the future. After being indoctrinated, his family would be notified, and he would be able to write to them.

Johnny finally agreed not to resist and was told he could get up off the floor and sit on one of the seats with the other boys. Johnny thought he would wait for the opportunity to escape but for now he would agree not to cause any more problems for the two soldiers on guard in the wagon. He could tell that both soldiers had no patience with their current assignment and would not hesitate to be as physical as need be to keep peace in the wagon.

There were so many questions he wanted to ask but he kept silent, so he could concentrate and try to memorize the route and direction they were traveling. Johnny was not like the other captive occupants of the cart. Looking around, he thought he was somewhat older and physically stronger than the other boys. Although he was young in age, he was shown how to use weapons, hunt, and ride horses. He would go on hunting trips with his father and brother and learned to survive the elements earlier than most of the farm children. Yes, he would try to escape and make it back to his village, but now was not the time to do so.

The caravan traveled for hours and only stopped to allow those needing to relieve themselves on the side of the road. They were under guard at all times. The sun was going down and they stopped at a very large open area to set up camp and attend a chow line. Tents were set up and the captives were given blankets and led into a large tent to rest for the night under guard.

He was tired and fell asleep with thoughts and concern for his family. When will they be informed of the situation? He knew they will be worried, and he wanted them to know that he was alive and not able to come home. The days passed with relatively the same routine. Johnny still felt that he was capable of tracking his way back home.

After what seemed like a lifetime, the column finally turned off the main road. They entered a very large military encampment. They were led to a small wooded structure with mattresses on the floor. They were assigned to their sleeping area and given mess kits.

A soldier with a deep and gruff voice came in with two other soldiers to tell them what was expected from them. They first were told one of the captives had tried to escape and was shot and killed. Johnny was not sure if he believed the story but thought he should be careful and not share his plans to escape with any of the other captives. They were given their assignments and Johnny was relieved. Some of the boys were assigned to mess duties and other assignments which did not interest him. He was assigned to care for the horses in the stable. He could do this. He loved horses. They wanted his name and the names of everyone who lived in his home, their relationship to him, and where he lived. They did this in order to notify his family. He gave his full name: Johnny Santoro.

The soldier writing down his profile looked at him when he heard Johnny say his surname was Santoro.

"Do you know what your name means?" He said.

Johnny answered, "I don't understand."

The soldier then told him. "Sant means Saint and oro means Gold." From now on, I am going to call you Young *Johnny Saint Gold.* You will give the regiment good luck!"

From that time on everyone that had anything to do with Johnny fondly referred to him as Johnny Saint Gold. The Sergeant that was in charge of the regimental stable also was named John. He was a tall man with a large frame. Since both were familiar faces to anyone who had business in the stable, they called the Sergeant "Big John." and young Johnny was called, "Johnny Saint Gold."

Days passed, and Johnny worked hard tending the horses. His efforts did not go unnoticed. Big John liked what he saw in Johnny and soon he was given special liberties. Big John often asked Johnny to join him to ride around the camp. Young Johnny had settled in and thought to himself that he should not be in any rush to leave for home. They trusted him, and he could leave any time he wanted to. Everyone treated him well and he was rubbing elbows with the soldiers when they came in the stables to pick up their mounts. He also liked being called Johnny Saint Gold.

There were spare horses that were not yet assigned to anyone and Johnny was given the job of working them out each day. This got him away from other less desirable duties like cleaning out the stables. He was spending most of the day mounted and he loved it.

Johnny would get information from the soldiers who visited the stables on what was rumored to happen before word of the event would come down through proper channels. He often knew before Big John, but of course never told him he already knew what Big John was about to tell him.

Rumor was that the Regiment would soon go south again, and Johnny had to think what he should do about trying to escape and returning home.

Then one day Big John handed Johnny a letter. It was from home. He opened the envelope quickly to read what his family wrote. They were told that

Johnny was now a member of the military and was assigned to a non-combative job. The government said that they were soliciting adult recruits and until their roster requirement was completed, Johnny needed to stay. They assured his parents that he would be well fed and properly cared for and that he would be returned home as soon as possible. His father told Johnny to be brave and not try to return home since they were warned that a severe penalty would be imposed if he did.

Johnny felt sad but knew he could cope with the situation and he liked everyone he worked with. He would hang in there. He would be able to return home soon and he wanted to be brave.

Big John was like a big brother and they spent a lot of spare time together. He was married without children and told Johnny that if he had a boy, he wanted him to be just like Johnny.

Several days later the Regiment was ordered to move south. Getting ready for the task was no easy matter. But soon they were on the march again. By now, Johnny stopped watching for clues as to where they were going and how to back track home. He would do his duty and make his family proud. He would return home someday. He would eventually see them again – or so he thought.

They traveled many miles each day and would stop at rest locations to make camp every night. The government had kept their word. Some of the other youngsters assigned to mess duties were returned home since they were relieved by new adult replacements.

Johnny asked Big John, "Why were they released and not me?"

"Most anyone can be replaced but you have done a great job taking care of the stable," Big John said. "Working out the horses as well as you do, it is not easy to find a replacement for you."

"Have patience, more replacements are on the way. I know you want to go home. I want you to be happy, but I will miss you when you are replaced, my young friend." Johnny actually felt good having Big John praise him.

The Regiment continued to move south. Several weeks passed and there were no rumors about where they were going. Johnny asked many of the soldiers that had given him information before. No one had heard anything. All they knew was that they were continuing to head south. Wherever they were headed was meant to be kept secret. The Regiment intensified training sessions. Caring of the horses now required even more work hours. Johnny was very tired in the evening and fell asleep as soon as he laid down to rest. In the past, he would have trouble falling asleep. He would think of the farm and his family and what had happened to him.

Johnny wrote to his family after he received their first letter, but as time passed, he had trouble finding the time and effort with his increased workload. He was becoming accustomed to his new life as a young soldier.

He did not want his family to worry and thought that he should try to write to them more often.

One day Big John visited the stable with an older officer and introduced Johnny to him. The officer's name was Captain De Mateo. The Captain shook Johnny's hand and said to him, "So you are Johnny Saint Gold. It is rumored that you will bring luck to the Regiment and that you have done a great job with the horses."

Captain De Mateo walked around to inspect the stable with Big John. As he was leaving, he looked in Johnny's direction and gestured to Johnny a half salute goodbye. Johnny again felt that his hard work was appreciated.

The next day, the Regiment was on the move again. That evening, the column reached another camp and set up for mess call and a night's rest. The horses had to be fed, watered and rubbed down by Johnny and the crew in the stables. In the morning, Johnny noticed there was something different about this place. The air was humid, and his shirt was damp from a mist that settled on the camp. There were large white birds flying over, all making sounds that were unfamiliar to him.

Big John arrived and told him, "We are near a seaport town and the orders were to embark on a ship and they would have to lead the horses on board."

He said that it would take most of the day to load all the horses and equipment. Big John still did not know where the final destination was.

Johnny had many questions he wanted to ask Big John, but everything was hectic. Captain De Mateo and Big John took charge of the movement of the horses and related equipment, so Johnny was not able to privately ask Big John all the questions he needed to ask him.

His mind kept going over the questions. *"When is he going home? Will they send him home before the ship is loaded or will he have to board the ship? Where is the ship going? Is it far?"* He wanted to get to Big John alone. Surely, he would have to do it before the ship is loaded and all were aboard.

One of the other soldiers helping with the move said to Johnny, "The white birds are called seagulls." As the column approached the town, many more seagulls were flying around, and the air smelled of fish and salt. Johnny sighted the water and the ships that had already started to load equipment. There were many ships being loaded. He had never seen anything like this.

Finally, Big John approached and said, "I know you have a lot of questions to ask but I want you to trust me. I was not informed of the voyage in advance. I still do not know the final destination of the cruise. Johnny, you will have to board with the others and we will talk on the ship once everyone is on board."

Johnny was confused, but he did trust Big John. He really did not have a choice. Each soldier attended to his own mount and led his horse up the gang plank of the ship. Along with other help, Johnny would do the same for each of the spare horses previously held in reserve in the stable.

Johnny did not have the chance to write to his family before boarding the ship. How would he get a letter to them now? If he could send them a letter, he would have to tell them he did not know where he was going. The ships sailed away to destinations unknown. His mind was having thoughts of regret. Maybe he should have tried to escape after they first began to trust him, when he had the opportunity of doing so. He could have escaped after he became friends with Big John. Over and over in his mind Johnny thought he waited too long to make his move. Then he thought of the letter he first received when his father said, "Do not try to come home." A severe penalty could be imposed if he did and there was no place to hide or go if he escaped successfully. Johnny had to face the fact that he had to be brave and count on his relationship with Big John to survive.

Chapter Three

A Voyage to Africa

Life on the ship was terrible and boring. It was hard to clean the stable area and also hard to groom and feed the horses. Much time was spent on keeping them calm in their confined area. The only good benefit about being on the ship was that Johnny had more time to spend with Big John.

He explained to young Johnny, "Everything relative to both our lives in the military is controlled by those commanding above my rank. I will do my best to keep you safe and watch over you as long as we are together." Johnny was comforted by this promise.

Eighteen-Hundreds Dockside

"I am eager to visit your family and farm someday and tell them how brave you are," said Big John. Johnny did not answer, he only smiled. He had come to really like Big John and viewed him as a father figure.

Johnny told him about each member of his family and how he learned to ride and hunt with his father and brother and about his prize horse "Bella."

"There is a tan colt in the stable reserve that reminds me of Bella," Johnny said without expectation.

Big John responded in a way that surprised Johnny. "Consider the tan colt yours. I will assign it to you when we depart from the ship."

The stable reserves were horses that were not assigned to any particular soldier. They would be used as a replacement if there were any problems with a soldier's assigned mount or when a new recruit joined the regiment and needed a mount. Johnny was about to get his very own horse!

Suddenly a view of land appeared in the distance. Everyone on board was told they should be prepared to land. The port ahead was slowly approached by this large armada of ships. Their ship reduced its speed and proceeded to dock. It took a while to pull up to the pier. There were many other boats waiting to land loaded with additional militia and equipment. The order to leave the ship was given and occupants and equipment proceeded to leave the ship in an orderly manner.

They left the landing area and proceeded to move in a direction away from the water. Their destination was a very large military encampment just beyond the seaport town. As the column moved through the town, they saw the native residents who were dressed in hats called turbans and they wore long robes. Their skin was dark and many of them had large curved swords strapped to their sides. They finally reached the encampment and the regiment settled in. The horses were fed and seemed much calmer with their hoofs on land again.

There was a briefing that evening and Johnny was told that no one was allowed to leave the camp. They were told they had landed in Africa and they were facing a battle with the Ethiopian army. Big John was informed that this Regiment and other units that came over on the boats would join up tomorrow and move out to join with the main Italian forces commanded by General Baratieri. The main force, when consolidated with this Regiment, would consist of approximately four brigades, seventeen thousand men, and fifty artillery pieces.

They would join the main force just north of a town called Adwa. The Regiment moved out and eventually met with General Baratieri's forces. They were integrated into one of the general's brigades.

Big John told Johnny that he wanted him to ride and stay close by his side. He told him not to worry. The Italian militia was a very formidable force. Little Johnny had seen them train and knew that Big John was correct. Johnny thought that if he was not so afraid, he would almost feel sorry for the enemy. "We will get through this skirmish and return home safe and sound. Have faith," said Big John.

They were told they would engage the Ethiopian army with a surprise attack very early the next morning. Johnny had lost memory of time and date. He wanted to remember to tell his parents the date of this extraordinary event in his life when he returned home. He had a small notebook and pencil in his pocket. There was not much information written in the notebook. He was going to use it to record notes to backtrack home, but it was never used for that purpose.

He kept it in his pocket hoping to start a diary of events someday. He opened the notebook and wrote *"March 1, 1896 - The Battle of Adwa…"*

Chapter Four
Into Battle

Johnny had never imagined being in such a dangerous situation. He was not an adult, and still very much a child. What in the world was he doing here away from his mother, father, his family, and his home? He was about to be involved in a battle. The military had forgotten their promise to send him home. *Did someone loose his paperwork? Was it misfiled? This is not fair. This is not right!*

Big John had repeatedly questioned his superiors relative to when young Johnny would be replaced and returned home. Each time they told him that they had asked headquarters and were told that there were still not enough enlistees available for combative duties due to the military involvement in Africa. Children old enough to do other duties were still needed. Big John thought that this was an administrative screw-up. Young Johnny should not be here.

Unknown to Johnny, a conflict originated in 1893 over a treaty signed by the Emperor of Ethiopia and Italy. The bilingual Treaty did not specify the same terms when translated in the Italian copy as the terms in the Ethiopian copy relative to control over an area called Eritrea in the northeast of Ethiopia. A chain of events and military conflict over the interpretation of the treaty shaped the future destiny of young Johnny Saint Gold.

The regiment met with the main force at approximately four in the morning of the attack and took their assigned position on the right flank somewhat to the rear. Big John said that they were positioned not to see frontal exposure to the initial attack but to protect the right flank of the main army. He assured young Johnny that all should go well.

Johnny was riding very close to Big John on the tan mount that Big John had assigned to him. The horse reminded him of his own horse on the farm. He also named his new horse Bella. He was given a standard issue rifle. Big John was aware that Johnny could handle the rifle since they often practiced together on a firing range when they were on the Italian mainland.

General Baratieri had been informed that the Ethiopians had massed a larger force, so he wanted to mount a surprise attack early in the morning while the enemy was asleep. The Ethiopians woke even earlier for church services and were warned of the advance of the Italian Army. The Ethiopians with a militia of over 100,000 and 50 artillery pieces initiated the attack first.

The Regiment saw what they thought was infantry approaching to the right flank of their columns, so they were ordered to stop and turn right to face the oncoming troops. They were told not to fire or attack until they were ordered to do so. Big John told Johnny to position himself behind him. It was still not clear why infantry would try to attack mounted cavalry.

As they came closer it was clear that this was not an infantry attack. It appeared that they were Arab civilians. They looked to be mostly women and children lined up side-by-side, all parallel to the mounted column. It was thought that they were trying to get away from the fighting up ahead since Johnny's regiment was somewhat behind the main force, but they were coming toward the right flank of the mounted procession. They should be heading to the rear. They did not appear to be armed and the order was issued to let them pass through. This proved to be a fatal mistake for many that day.

A cloud of dust appeared far in the direction that the civilians came from. It looked like a sand storm. The next event created havoc among the mounted militia. While the women and children infiltrated the mounted ranks to pass through, they uncovered and pulled out long curved swords hidden from beneath their gowns. They started hacking at the legs of the horses and soldiers. Many horses went down throwing their riders. Many of the soldier's legs were hacked and they fell off their mounts. The soldiers were ordered to shoot them, but it was already too late. Blood was splashed over everyone. Some of the ankles of both soldiers and horses were completely severed.

Battle of Adwa Painting

The approaching so-called sand storm turned out to be the Ethiopian cavalry. They hit the regiment in large numbers and inflicted enormous casualties. It was sword-to-sword fighting.

Big John yelled to Johnny, "Turn your horse around now and get the hell out of here!"

As Johnny turned his horse to run, he noticed an Arab approaching him on his left with his sword raised high, ready to strike him. He was so close that Johnny could see his rotten teeth and smell his body odor. Johnny kicked into the sides of his mount, put his head down and road the horse hard. He expected to be killed by the Arab's sword at any moment. He did not turn around and did not stop until the horse could no longer run and was covered with foam. He found himself alone in the desert.

Johnny got off his horse and looked back in the direction he came from. No Arab. No Big John. There was no one. He was all alone. The sun was hot and high in the sky. He guessed it was probably close to noontime. He was covered with blood but was not wounded. He took a taste of water from his canteen and with the palm of his hand gave his horse a drink. He thought he would have to conserve his water. He had no idea what was ahead.

He wondered what happened to the Arab who was about to hack him from behind. Someone must have killed him and saved Johnny's life. It could have been Big John.

He started walking and thought. "I am lost and do not know where I am going. I lost my protector Big John and now I am all alone." He felt the rapid beat of his heart. He was afraid to be alone in this foreign place. From the time he was captured, he always had someone to guide him.

He cried out loud, "Oh God, please help me!"

He took his jacket off and hung it over the saddle. He knew he would need it at night when it got cold. He walked the horse slowly and stroked Bella's forehead. Moments later a call rang out from someone far in the distance. Johnny could hardly see who they were. It looked like three people with four horses. They were waving but he could not tell if they were Italians or Arabs and he could not understand what they were yelling. He stood motionless while they came closer. Were they friends or foe? His life's journey was about to take yet another remarkable turn.

Chapter Five
All Aboard to America

As they approached, young Johnny saw to his delight, they were Italian militia. It appeared that they were alone and probably as lost as he was.

They shook Johnny's hand and introduced themselves to him. There was a tall soldier named Angelo. The other two men were named Frank and Nick. He was relieved they were friendly.

"I was a baker working in my father's bakery before I joined the military," said Nick as he extended his hand for a friendly handshake. He said he had planned on opening his own bakery when his military term was over. "My family owns a cafe and I plan on going back to work in the family's business when all this is over," said Frank. Angelo hesitated a bit when Johnny asked what he did before he joined the military.

He smiled and said, "I was a banker."

Johnny sensed that there was more to Angelo than met the eye, but this was not the time to ask a lot of questions. Johnny told them all about the battle including why he had dried blood all over his hands, face and uniform. He told them how the Arab women and children had infiltrated the mounted ranks with hidden swords and started hacking at the feet of the mounted soldiers and their horses. He told them that the Arab cavalry had then attacked them. It was a complete disaster and how he was lucky to escape alive.

Angelo told Johnny that the three of them had no intention of going back to the Italian Army. Before the attack they were told where to regroup if necessary, for another counter attack. They were all through risking their lives against overwhelming odds. The battle was a disaster and the Italians were completely outnumbered. The Ethiopians were extremely dedicated in defending their country.

By afternoon, the four brigades of the Italian militia were partially destroyed and in full retreat, scattered throughout the area. This was not the first campaign against the Ethiopians which Angelo, Frank, and Nick had been involved in. All three of them had fought at Amba Alagi on December 7, 1895 when again overwhelming numbers of the Ethiopian Army forced the Italians to retreat back to Eritea.

The three of them had planned to desert and they would never be able to go back to their homes and family in Italy. They would rather be alive to make a new life somewhere else, than go back and risk their lives again in what they thought was a losing cause. Angelo said he had a plan and knew approximately where they were. He was familiar with the area because of his prior experience in campaigning against the Ethiopians.

Johnny was invited to join them. On the other hand, if Johnny wanted to rejoin the scattered forces to regroup for another attack, Angelo would point him in the direction he should go. He left the choice to Johnny.

Johnny did not know what he should do. If he tried to regroup with the retreating Italian militia, he might have to participate in another attack. He no longer had Big John to look over and protect him. By now, he was convinced that most of his Regiment was destroyed and that Big John was killed. He was lucky he was alive. If he regrouped, he may not survive to see his family again. The military had no regard for him and he did not owe them anything. Maybe they would think he was killed. In that case, he may be able to make his way home again to see his family. But what would happen if the authorities found out that he survived and was found at home. He would be punished as a deserter.

Johnny was confused and knew whatever decision he made there could cause problems. If only he could ask his father what he should do. If only Big John was alive and with him now.

He discussed his dilemma with Angelo and asked for his advice. He told Angelo every detail of his journey from the start of his capture to the big battle when Big John told him to race away. When the discussion was over, Angelo put his hand on Johnny's shoulder and told him he was a very brave young boy and that he admired him.

Angelo said that he did not believe he would be as brave as Johnny if the situation was reversed and he was at Johnny's age with the same chain of events. Johnny beamed. He told Johnny he would look after him as Big John did if he wanted to join them.

Angelo's plan was to head for a seaport in Entrea, Africa which became an official colony of Italy on January 1st, 1890. They would seek passage on a ship going to Spain or Portugal, or even South America - any place far away from Italy. They could make new lives and write to their families to tell them that they were alive and well. He said he had lots of Italian lira and local currency in his saddlebags and told him that he would explain how he happened to have all this money in his possession when they got to their destination.

"We need to get to a seaport town where Italian and local money is circulated. This requires a port that is used to receive and dispatch Italian ships including military transports and internationally bound civilian freighters," said Angelo, outlining a plan. "There will be risks so we have to cover our uniforms and dress like the local Arabs."

He told him when they got to the seashore not to wash their faces and hands. The blood from the battle had given Johnny a dark dry skin and he looked like an Arab. Johnny liked Angelo, Frank, and Nick. They all looked up to Angelo. He would be their leader. Johnny agreed to go with them and not try to return to regroup with the Regiment. He only hoped that this was the right decision for him to make. His decision would later prove to save his life in more ways than one.

Although Angelo, Frank, and Nick were willing to help young Johnny if he went with them, they could not disclose that they would not allow him to rejoin the Regiment. They worried that he would possibly tell of their plan to dessert. They had to protect their lives even if this meant eliminating Johnny. They were glad he decided to go with them. They were no longer faced with the possibility of killing Johnny.

They followed Angelo and he quickly proved that he indeed knew where he was going and could lead them to freedom. They met a caravan of Arab merchants on the way and Angelo was able to trade the extra horse for some food and water. The merchants wanted the horse until they noticed that it was branded with a military symbol. Angelo told them he was authorized to sell the horses when they were not needed. Angelo would sign a bill of sale to substantiate the merchants had purchased the horse from him in trade for water and food.

The merchants had doubts, but it only cost them some food and water. They knew that if they put a blanket over the rump of the horse, no one could see the military brand.

Angelo also purchased turbans, robes and blankets from the merchants using some of the money in the saddlebags. The blankets would keep them warm at night. The head pieces and robes would be worn to go over their uniforms when they reach the seaport. The merchant wanted to trade for their rifles but now was not the time to rid themselves of their weapons.

What they did not know was that the Italian Military would eventually regroup and send everyone back to the Italian homeland. If Johnny, Angelo, Frank, and Nick had actually returned to the militia, they would have been eventually sent home. There was no reason they would be exposed to another battle. The casualty losses for the Italian forces at the battle of Adwa were estimated to be more than any other European battle of the 19th century. The Italian civilian populace was extremely angry with the government which soon collapsed due to its failures in military involvement in Africa. Italy was now at peace. Italy returned to stage war on the Ethiopian Empire again (years later in 1935 and 1936). Ethiopia was defeated, put under Italian military rule and occupation until the defeat of Italy in the East African Campaign of World War II in 1941.

They approached the sea town, decided to ditch the horses, and walked toward the port. They hid their weapons under their robes. Angelo removed the money from the saddle bags and wrapped it in a blanket. He found an inn for much-needed rest near a merchants' bazaar and purchased a suitable bag to carry the money. They were all exhausted. All they had to do now was sleep.

They slept well that night, although they were worried about being caught. There were many Italian soldiers walking around the bazaar the first night when Angelo picked up his money bag. Johnny felt they all had their eyes on the four of them. Looking in the mirror in their room, he looked very dark from the dried blood on his hands and face. Angelo again reminded him not to wash the blood off.

He said, "We should look for some type of lotion to darken our skin like Johnny's."

They went into the bazaar to shop, eat and quickly returned back to their lodging. Angelo wanted them to stay in their room until he had returned. It would be safer for all of them if only one person exposed themselves outside. He would go down to the docks and check out what options were available to them. He took the money bag with him, saying that he would scout what ships were docked and learn more about their destinations. He hopefully would find someone that he could trust that would help them - for a price of course. He was gone for a long time. Frank was the first to question Angelo's motives.

"Why did he take the money bag? Did he not trust us? Was it safe to go alone? Should one of us be with him to protect the money? Is he coming back or is he making arrangements for himself, leaving us to fend for ourselves?"

Johnny said, "Angelo would not do that."

"Johnny you are too young to understand," replied Frank.

Because of Frank's remarks, Johnny was starting to worry about his new friend Angelo.

"Where did he get all that money?" asked Johnny.

Nick replied, "Did you ask him?"

Johnny said, "He said he will tell me when we reach our destination. I think it is great that he is willing to spend his money to help us also."

Nick said, "Why not? It is not his money and he may decide not to return for us."

Johnny wondered again about the source of the money and began to worry that they had been deserted. All of them stopped talking and silently waited for the return of Angelo. Time passed, and nightfall approached. Their chances of ever seeing Angelo again diminished. Johnny thought of what he had gone through and what could happen to him if he were caught. He thought of home and not being able to tell his family that he was still alive and unable to return. He hoped he would be able to return home someday and explain to the authorities that he was young and had to take the advice of older, more mature advisors. Angelo told him he would never be able to return home again.

He hoped he was wrong. For now, he would have to follow Angelo's advice. He did not know what to do if Angelo did not return. Frank and Nick also looked up to Angelo as their leader. All would be lost without him.

It was late, and they all wondered if they should go to the dock and look for Angelo. It was dark, and he would be hard to find at night. They decided they should wait till the morning. They would have a better chance of finding him in the daylight. That evening they had a restless sleep. Morning came and still no sign of Angelo.

Frank and Nick had enough Italian liras on them to go to the bazaar to pick up some food. The merchants in the bazaar were used to dealing with Italian speaking customers and accepted Italian lira for goods since the Italian military used this port for troop landing and supplies. Still, Angelo had warned them not to leave the room before he returned, for fear of being exposed.

They were all hungry and it was decided that Johnny would stay and wait for Angelo. When they returned with food, they would discuss what to do if Angelo did not show up. Shortly after they left, Angelo finally returned. He was very tired. He was quite upset that they had left the room to go to the bazaar. Johnny was relieved to see him. Angelo said he made travel arrangements and he would explain more only when the other two had returned. Meanwhile, he needed to rest. Frank and Nick returned with food and found Angelo in a deep sleep. They waited for him to wake and were eager to hear what his plans were.

Angelo had made arrangements to board freighters which would leave the next evening. He had visited several bars along the port and overheard conversations. He met and befriended a fellow Italian named Nino who worked as a purser on a ship that would leave port the next evening for the Americas. He offered to pay Nino if he could get the four of them on board.

Nino thought that it would be difficult to arrange for all four. He could take two and ask his friend Joseph, who was on another ship leaving one hour earlier, if he could arrange to take the other two. Spain was the destination of Joseph's ship.

They hunted down Nino's friend Joseph and agreed on price and terms. They would all meet tomorrow at a bar at noon to finalize the plans. Angelo thought that he would team up with young Johnny and that Frank and Nick should go together on the other ship. Johnny was relieved that Angelo had picked him for his traveling partner.

Nick asked which two would go to Spain. Angelo said he did not care and that both destinations were far enough from Africa and Italy.

"I don't mind The Americas. What about you Johnny?"

Johnny never heard of The Americas or even Spain, for that matter.

"You decide," Johnny said, leaving his fate in the hands of Angelo. Not only did he trust Angelo, he trusted whatever decision Angelo would make.

"If everyone agrees, Johnny and I will go to The Americas and Frank and Nick will go to Spain," said Angelo, knowing that the others would agree. Angelo also agreed to split what was left of the money once the voyages were paid for.

The next day they all met Nino. They gave him a small deposit with the balance to be paid on the ships. This was a big risk, but they had to take it. A number of events could happen. The money could be stolen before they went on board. They could be turned into the authorities. Nino and Joseph could double cross them. One thing that gave them some faith was that Nick came from the same province as Joseph and they both knew of distant relatives of their families. They were fellow countryman. Everyone felt a little more relaxed.

That evening, they met on the dock in a dark secluded area and were ready to board the ships. Angelo and Johnny shook hands with Nick and Frank and wished each other good luck. They each had the mailing address of Johnny's family in Avellino. They all promised to write to Johnny's father Dominic to report their safe journey out of Italian jurisdiction and how they could be reached to communicate with each other in the future.

Johnny watched Nick and Frank leave with Joseph for their ship. He could not help feeling sad to see them go. They had formed a strong relationship. Johnny wondered if he would ever see them again. Would they be safe? Would he be safe?

Nino led Angelo and Johnny to their vessel. It was dark, and Nino told them to move quickly and to be very quiet. Before long they were below deck in a room where goods and water were stored.

"This would be your home till the end of the voyage," said Nino.

Nino was actually related to the Captain. He told them that the Captain knew that they were aboard and shared in the payment that Angelo gave Nino for their passage. He told them that the captain wanted them to stay below deck during the day, but they could come on deck in the evening to get fresh air.

Nino said that he would bring them food twice each day. They could remove the turbans and robes when they were below deck in the storage room, but he wanted them to wear them when they were on deck in the evening. Some of the crew were Arabs and they would blend in with them while on deck. There were fewer crew members on deck in the evenings. The crew was mainly comprised of Italians and Arabs. There was no real problem for Angelo and Johnny since the Captain was involved in their agreement.

Chapter Six
A Flight to Freedom

The first week aboard was uneventful. Nino brought them food as he promised, and the only problem was boredom and the feeling of captivity. They told each other stories of their home and families. Angelo had been in trouble with the law on several occasions prior to joining the military. Johnny liked Angelo and felt he was lucky to have him as a friend and counselor. He wondered what he would do if he did not have Angelo in his situation. Days passed, then weeks passed. Johnny got sick and eventually Angelo got sick as well. Both of them had dysentery. Johnny expressed his concern that they may not make it to the Americas.

"Be strong and have faith," said Angelo with conviction.

One evening Angelo felt very ill and did not feel strong enough to go up on deck. Johnny said he would go up and let Angelo rest, but Angelo did not want Johnny to go up on deck alone. Johnny insisted and went up anyway. He sat on a bench breathing the fresh sea air. Two Italian speaking men approached Johnny and sat on either side of him. One started talking to him.

"Little man, who are you and what are you doing here?"

Johnny did not answer him. He thought it best to be quiet.

The man said to the other man, "He looks Arab and I don't think he understands us."

"Little man come with us. We will show you where we work below deck."

Meanwhile Nino dropped in to visit Angelo to see how he was feeling. Angelo told Nino that Johnny went above deck alone and he was gone for a long time.

Would he please go above and check on him?

The two men grabbed Johnny under his armpits and started to pull him up from his sitting position. Johnny tried to resist but the men were able to drag him across the deck toward

Vintage Ocean Crossing Steamship

the stairway below. Johnny continued to resist. One of the men turned to face Johnny and slapped him hard across the face. Johnny had his hard leather sole riding boots on under his robe and kicked him in the knee causing him to grimace with pain. The other man threw a punch at Johnny's face. It missed its intended mark, but hit his shoulder causing Johnny to grunt with pain. Johnny tried to kick him in the leg but missed and his boot landed dead center up his groin. The man doubled over in pain.

Johnny ran, and the two men were about to follow him when Nino appeared and called to Johnny. They knew Nino and his relationship with the Captain, so they left quickly in the opposite direction. Needless to say, Johnny never went on deck alone for the rest of the trip. Mercifully, it was just a few days later Nino told them they were not far from land.

The vessel prepared to pull into port. "We will land in a place called New York but not the usual landing port for immigrants called Ellis Island," Nino told them. "The ship will unload freight in another New York Port busied with other commercial ships. I will lead you off the ship one-at-a-time once unloading is started."

Nino told them that he would take young Johnny first and then come back for Angelo. His plan was to avoid Customs by pretending to help unload packages to the docking platform. The packages were placed in an area which was closed off and surrounded by rope and connecting posts approximately three feet high and eight feet apart. The only open access to the area was from the ramp coming off the ship. It would be easy to get out of the storage area by bending down and quickly crawling under the rope while no one was looking. There was a Customs inspector at the bottom of the ramp. He inspected everyone leaving the ship. The inspector would allow the crew to enter the storage area and then allow them to return to the ship to pick up more packages. The inspector would be very busy interviewing people leaving the ship, so he would be somewhat distracted to what was happening in the storage area.

"After you are free from the storage area, you will see a six-foot metal link fence straight ahead. Turn left and follow the fence. At the very end climb over the fence and you will be at the front entrance of the terminal," Nino told them, outlining the rest of the plan. Angelo would follow and soon catch up to Johnny. Providing everything went as planned, they would start their new life in the new world.

Nino shook their hands and they thanked him for all he had done. It was time to leave the ship. Johnny followed Nino and wondered what would happen if he was stopped by the inspector. Would he be sent back to Italy and punished for desertion?

Johnny helped Nino unload a package, going down the ramp and placing it in the storage area. Without any hesitation to look back at Nino or the inspector, he slipped under the rope and headed for the metal link fence. He was nervous. He had the

New York Waterfront

same fear when Big John told him to turn and race away during the battle. He thought again about being chased by the Arab with his sword ready to strike him.

The fence was just ahead. Now, he thought he must turn left as Nino had instructed and follow the fence to the end. He turned to the left and walked at a quick step. He was so nervous. He thought again of what Nino said. *Did he say turn left or did he say turn right at the fence?* He tried to concentrate but felt panic and could not remember. Should he continue or go back for Angelo? He could stop and wait for him. He decided to continue and wait for him at the end of the fence. He eventually reached the end and looked back. Where was Angelo? He must come soon. Time passed, and Johnny thought Angelo must have been stopped or perhaps turned right at the fence. In any case, he was all alone in this new and strange place. He thought of walking back and turning himself into customs. He had enough!

On the other side of the fence he heard a conversation between two men and a woman. One man spoke English which Johnny could not understand. Later he learned English was the native language of this country. The other man and woman also spoke English, but occasionally spoke Italian to each other. The three of them finished their conversation and one of the men left. The man and women stayed and continued to talk to each other in Italian. They were about to leave when Johnny yelled out to them. He did not know what else to do.

"Can you please help me?" He was still more a child than a man, and halfway across the world. He was alone and scared, and his voice quivered.

The man came closer to the opposite side of the fence and said, "Who are you and what do you want from us?"

Johnny still had his turban and robe on. He still had dried blood staining his face and hands. Angelo told him not to remove the stains, so he would look darker.

The man asked. "What is your nationality and how do you know how to speak Italian?"

Johnny started to tell him of his plight from the time he was captured near his home by the militia to his present situation. Tears rolled down his cheeks and he tried hard not to sob. The woman came closer to the fence. He tried not to leave anything out. His voice was shaking. The man told him to slow down. He was talking too fast. Johnny finished his tale of events. Their names were Carmen and Rose Pelosi. They listened and seemed to be genuinely interested in Johnny's plight. Johnny broke down and he cried. He tried to control himself, but the emotions blocked from his recent experiences burst open like a floodgate.

Johnny looked at both of them and said, "Please help me. I do not know what to do. My mother and my father are in Italy. I will work hard for you if you help me. I think my friend Angelo was caught getting off the ship. I need to get away from this place before they catch me."

Mr. and Mrs. Pelosi turned to each other and had a private conversation in English.

Then Mr. Pelosi turned back to Johnny. "Can you climb over this fence?" he asked.

Johnny started to climb and felt someone was pulling him down. He panicked and turned to look back. His robe got caught on the fence. He was able to get his robe free, continue to climb over the fence and land on the other side. Mr. and Mrs. Pelosi led Johnny out of the terminal. Johnny's new life in America was about to begin.

Chapter Seven
Welcome to America

At the time that they met young Johnny, Rose and Carmen Pelosi were in their mid-forties. They had two daughters, twelve-year-old Donna and fourteen-year-old Lucy. The Pelosi's were on vacation in New York City when they met young Johnny. Carmen built residential homes and they lived in upstate New York at that time.

Johnny often thought about Angelo and Big John, and all the other people who crossed his path during his long journey. He had tried to wash the dried blood off his hands and face after he thankfully joined up with the Pelosi family. The blood had adhered to his skin and was difficult to wash away with just soap and hot water.

The blood was so dry that when Johnny tried to peal it off as he soaked in the bathtub his skin peeled off along with the dry blood. Mr. Pelosi told him to leave it alone and repetitive soaking over time will eventually remove the blood. Mr. Pelosi seemed to know a lot about things. Johnny liked him immediately.

Johnny was to Mr. and Mrs. Pelosi the son they never had. He was accepted into their family and was cared for and loved as if he was their biological son. They were kind and compassionate. Johnny was very fortunate that destiny led him to them.

He wrote to his family to tell them that he was safe in the United States. He told them all about his good fortune to be living with the Pelosi family. His father wrote back and told Johnny how happy they all were that he was safe. His father wrote that the authorities made a visit to the farm looking for Johnny and said he would be tried as a deserter if they found him. They took his brother Anthony into the military to serve out the rest of the military service that Johnny was responsible for. Johnny felt sick after he read the letter. He loved his brother Anthony and felt he now was responsible for whatever happened to Anthony while in the service.

Johnny was home-schooled by Mrs. Pelosi and helped Mr. Pelosi in his home building business. He became quite skilled at most of the laborious building trades, becoming an accomplished mason and carpenter. He always contributed some of his earnings to the Pelosi household in kind for their love and acceptance. He knew that he would never forget what they have done for him. They loved them as if they were his blood relatives.

He often thought of his family in Italy and hoped someday he would be able to earn enough money to bring them all to America. He loved his new country and wanted them to see and to be able to appreciate everything that America offered.

His family wrote to him often. They told him that Frank and Nick kept in touch with them and were glad Johnny was safe. Nick was working in a bakery and Frank got a job in a restaurant in Spain. This was good news. Angelo also wrote to check on Johnny. He told Dominic that he was caught and retained by the authorities when he got off the boat in New York. He had escaped and was now free in America. He asked Dominic to inform Johnny that he was glad to hear that he was safe and that he would also keep in touch through Dominic.

His brother Anthony had returned home from the service and wrote to Johnny often. He wrote Johnny that he did not blame him for his forced enlistment in the service when Johnny left the military. Anthony told Johnny that he was stationed in Italy for his term in the Italian army. His service time was peaceful, and he could often go home on leave.

He also told Johnny that the Italian people called for a change in the government after Italy's military loss in the battle of Adwa. Anthony was discharged from the service. Dominic fell ill, and Anthony took over the responsibilities of running the family farm. Anthony wanted to join Johnny someday in America. Both Johnny and Anthony wanted their mother, father, and sister to accompany Anthony to America. The plan was to wait for Dominic's health to improve, then sell the farm and move the family to America. Though that was their plan, Dominic remained in poor health for a very long time. The strain was great on the whole family. Johnny's mother started to have some health problems as well.

Years passed, and Johnny developed into a strong, tall, and handsome young man. A relative of Mr. and Mrs. Pelosi worked in a nearby steel mill and was able to get Johnny a job working there. The pay was good, and Johnny wanted to make more money to pay the Pelosi's for his board and to send money home to his family in Italy.

Working in a steel mill was an education in itself for Johnny. In a short time, Johnny developed muscles everywhere. He became strong and was given jobs only the strong could easily do.

He would bring a lunch in a paper bag and have his lunch just outside the mill building with several other workers. Johnny was a big eater and Mrs. Pelosi always packed a hefty lunch bag for him. She would make a sandwich using the whole loaf of Italian bread by slicing it down the side creating two large halves. She would then load it with cold cuts or sliced chicken or meatballs. Whatever she cooked or created to eat was great. She was a good cook just like his real mom Phyllis in Italy.

Chapter Eight
Workplace Conflict

One lunch time he was eating his very large sandwich while accompanied by his coworkers when another worker looked at Johnny and said, "Hey guinea wop what is that crap you're eating? Break off half of that garbage for me. I like to taste what you dagos eat."

Johnny had been brought up by both Dominic and Mr. Pelosi to stay out of trouble. He liked his job and did not want to lose it over a stupid squabble like this. He said nothing, trying to avoid a conflict. Johnny was tall, and well-built. He sized up the other fellow as being about the same size and of similar stature.

"I will come over there and take it all away from you - you stupid dago wop," said the man. Johnny still said nothing.

The man moved closer and reached out with his right hand to grab the sandwich while pushing Johnny back with his left hand. The sandwich dropped to the ground. Johnny closed his fists.

Suddenly a loud voice rang out, "Knock it off you two." The supervisor in charge of Johnny's department jumped in to separate them. "No fighting on company property or on company hours. If you want to kill each other you're not going to do it here. Lunch is over, go inside and get back to your work."

Johnny was quite upset and knew this was not over. He returned to his job. Two hours later there was a fifteen-minute work break. He was approached by his supervisor, a man named Ray. He wanted to talk to

Johnny. He told Johnny that he was a good worker and he did not want to see him mess up his employment with the company. He also knew that the problem had to be resolved. The other man was named Fred. He had worked in his department and had been transferred when Johnny was hired. Johnny replaced him, and Fred decided that he was going to get even with Johnny for taking his job.

Ray told Johnny that the only way this should be settled would be a fair fight between the two of them. Ray worked part time in the evenings as a sparring partner in a small gym nearby and would try to arrange for a fight for Johnny and Fred in a ring with gloves on. He would approach Fred to see if he agreed to fight. Ray would set the fight up.

"I am eager to knock the guinea wop's head off," said Fred enthusiastically.

Ray would get back to both of them and arrange the time and date.

"Have you ever fought with gloves before?" Ray asked Johnny one day.

"Never," replied Johnny. "Is there anything I should know about fighting with gloves?"

"Why don't you visit the gym tonight and I will go over everything with you," said Ray.

Johnny went to the gym that evening and saw Ray sparring with someone. He thought, "Why gloves?" He had fought with bare hands when he was younger and was somewhat puzzled with the use of gloves. Ray finished his sparring and got out of the ring to greet John.

"Why the gloves?" asked Johnny, genuinely confused.

Ray replied, "Boxing is a big sport in America and the gloves now allow fighters to last longer in the ring for the spectators than bare knuckles. A fighter can still be hurt badly if he does not have the stamina and if he cannot take a punch."

Ray showed him all the equipment in the gym and gave Johnny some hints while sparring with him for a short time. He told Johnny that he could use the gym in the evening for the next week if he wanted to. Ray needed the ring to be available. He did not have to pay for the use of the ring, as long as it was not being used by paying members. The ring would be available next week at 10:00 PM. It was late, but most of the members would have left the gym by that late hour.

Johnny really wanted to win, so he went to the gym every night before the fight and worked out on the punching bag, and other exercise equipment not being used by regular gym members.

Ray did not work every evening, but the evenings that both of them were there, he gave Johnny suggestions. He coached him to protect himself, to duck and move around the ring.

He said, "Hit Fred's belly and ribs hard, like you're hitting the punching bag. Aim for his face and stay off the ropes. Take advantage if you have him pinned to the ropes. He will throw wild punches if he has never boxed before. Protect yourself. Pace yourself. I will have to stop the fight if I feel one of you has been beaten and cannot continue to fight."

Johnny got the impression that Ray liked him and that he really wanted him to beat Fred.

Most of the other workers who knew Fred said he did not like Italians. He felt they came over from Italy to take jobs away from American workers.

Word quickly spread around the mill about the upcoming fight. Bets were made on both Johnny and Fred. Johnny could not believe he was thrown into a situation like this, a fight that he did not want to happen. He was forced into the fight, and the more he thought about it, the angrier he got.

The night before the fight, He visited the gym and punched the bag as hard as he could. He pictured the bag as Fred. He took his anger out on the bag. He thought, "Why all this hate in the world?"

He was so happy to be in America with Mr. and Mrs. Pelosi's family and now he had to worry again for his very survival. All he wanted was to work hard and look forward to the time that he could bring his family to America to join him. For as simple as his wishes were, life seemed to have other plans for Johnny.

Chapter Nine

Fight Night

Johnny was shocked when he entered the gym the night of the fight. The place was packed with workers from the mill. Johnny hoped Fred would not show up, but Fred walked in and headed straight for Johnny.

He practically put his face in Johnny's face and said, "I will beat your brains out tonight and every time I see you any place out of work, I will give you the same beating you are going to get tonight."

Ray greeted both Johnny and Fred and led them into the ring. He told them this would be a fight to the finish. There would be no rest breaks. The fight would continue until one fighter was down for good and could not continue. Before Ray even finished, both Johnny and Fred started to throw punches. The crowd was yelling, and both Johnny and Fred were swapping hard blows.

Johnny was hit a number of times in the face, as was Fred. It looked to be an even fight. Then Fred threw a wild right blow to Johnny's jaw forcing Johnny down on one knee. He got up quickly and received another blow to his left eye. Blood squirted out from an open slit just below the eye. He could not see clearly from that eye.

Johnny remembered what Ray said.," Hit Fred's belly and ribs hard like you're hitting a punching bag."

To do this he had to drop his fists and expose himself to more facial blows. He started to punch Fred in the belly and ribs hard with his left, then his right, over and over. He took a few more shots in the face from Fred, but he noticed that the harder he hit Fred in the midsection, the less power Fred's punches had. Johnny did not stop. He had Fred on the ropes. He kept pounding at Fred's midsection. Fred was hurting and dropped his arms to protect himself from Johnny's pulverizing body punches. Johnny saw an opening and started to throw punches at Fred's face. He hit Fred's nose and heard a noise like a snap. He had just broken

Amateur Boxing in Its Heyday

Fred's nose. Blood flowed all over Johnny's gloves. Johnny threw another right to Fred's right temple and he went down. Fred got back on his feet and Johnny threw a punch and hit his nose again. Fred went down hard and did not try to get up.

Ray grabbed Johnny, pulling him off Fred. "The fight is over," he announced to all.

Fred could not get up. Ray went over to attend to him. They sat him in a chair in a corner of the ring. Johnny's face was blood red and swollen all over. His left eye had closed shut and there was blood coming out of the cut below the eye. Ray brought Johnny over to Fred and said to them, "The fight is over, shake each other's hands."

No words were spoken. In fact, no words were ever spoken again between Fred and Johnny, although they would see each other from time-to-time from a distance at work. Fred eventually left the company for another job.

Johnny's coworkers greeted Johnny with raucous applause the next day. They liked Johnny and had made money betting on him. His face looked battered. But it was over, and Johnny was relieved. Hopefully no more fights, thought Johnny.

He thought the lecture he received from Mr. and Mrs. Pelosi was almost as emotionally severe as the actual fight. He did not want them to know about the fight but could not hide what his face looked like when he went home that night. John never thought he would see Mrs. Pelosi as upset as she was that night. She was always in a good mood and generally had a pleasant personality, but she was very angry at Johnny and let him know it. Rose did not hold back and told him repeatedly how disappointed she was over his fighting. She did not give him a chance to talk. Johnny looked towards Mr. Pelosi for support.

"Don't look at me," Mr. Pelosi said. "She is absolutely correct."

Rose loved Johnny and she felt meeting him for the first time at the opposite side of that fence in the ship terminal was a blessing for her. She lost her first child, a boy, during childbirth. Johnny filled the void created by that loss. Although she later gave birth to two healthy girls that she adored, Johnny needed to be cared for and she needed him. She could not imagine what would happen to their family without their son Johnny. She remembered Johnny's plea for help and her brief discussion with Carmen on the opposite side of the fence. She remembered telling Johnny to climb over the fence and into a new life in America. Her mind was baffled on what they would do when Johnny joined them on the other side of the fence, but they quietly led him out of the terminal and everything just fell into place.

Carmen joined in. "You are part of our family and when you are hurt, we all hurt. You have an obligation to your family here in America and to your family in Italy to keep yourself safe and from harm's way. That means not to get into fist fights, avoid confrontation, and try to act as a gentleman."

Johnny thought to himself, *"Both of you are not giving me a chance to explain. I was forced into it. If it was not for Ray, it would have been much worse. I will wait until things calm down and try to talk to them again and explain what happened that led to the fight."*

"You are both right. I am truly sorry for what I did and upsetting you both." Johnny said, meaning every word. He would do nothing to intentionally harm the Pelosi's.

Chapter Ten

Reunion Time

Back in Italy, Dominic and Phyllis did not age gracefully. They thought often of their son Johnny in America but would not discuss their sadness and the probability of never seeing him again. They had hoped that their health would improve, but that was not happening. They were grateful that Anthony was able to take charge of the farm. Their daughter Theresa was a great help maintaining the farmhouse by cooking and cleaning, all the while taking care of her aging mother and father. Anthony communicated with Johnny often by mail and kept him aware of what was happening with the family.

Anthony's friend Anna would come over often and kept company with him and the family. One day Anna made homemade ravioli and baked chicken for dinner and they were all ready to sit down at the table when visitors came to the farm. The gentleman introduced himself and his wife as Mr. and Mrs. Bonomo. He had one leg and used crutches. He was a very tall and handsome man. He said he had been a close friend of young Johnny in the military. Anthony invited them to join the family for dinner. He poured everyone a glass of homemade wine from a gallon jug sitting on the floor near his seat under the table. The wine was always at the ready for times just like this.

Mr. Bonomo asked about what had happened to young Johnny.

"Did he survive and return home?"

"He is well and in America," Dominic said. "What is your first name?" he then asked his unexpected visitor.

"John," he said. "They used to call me Big John."

Phyllis started to cry.

"Johnny had written often of you and how you looked after our boy when the military took him from us." Dominic said. "He thought you had not survived the battle."

"Your son was the bravest young boy I have ever seen. You all should be very proud of him. I had plans on visiting your home after I left the military, but it took a while for me to adjust to the fact that I left a part of myself in Africa. I have often thought of Johnny and wondered what happened to him."

Big John went on to tell them how well Johnny performed in the military and how he bravely rode side-by-side with Big John into battle.

By then, Dominic had tears in his eyes. "You do not know how much this means to us for you to come here today. Johnny will be very pleased to know that you have survived."

He wrote down Big John's address so that Johnny could write to him directly. Big John and his wife stayed for a while and the family enjoyed their company. They left after everyone hugged each other. By now, the two families had become one. Dominic and Phyllis again thanked him for taking care of their beloved son Johnny.

After Big John and his wife left, everyone thanked Anna for cooking a great dinner and Anthony accompanied her home. When he returned, they all sat around the table, had a glass of wine and talked about Big John's visit.

Dominic and Phyllis felt happy to hear Big John's comments about Johnny. It was long after their bedtime, but no one felt tired and it was apparent that they did not want this night to end. Anthony noted that for a number of years he had not seen his mother and father so happy. Everyone finally kissed each other goodnight and went to bed.

The next morning Anthony woke early, and Theresa woke shortly after. Theresa prepared breakfast and called Dominic and Phyllis to come down from their bedroom to eat. Dominic came down and sat at the table and covered his face in his hands and cried.

"What is wrong?" asked Theresa, worried about her father.

He could not answer.

She rushed up to her parent's bedroom. Upon entering, she saw her mother Phyllis looking like she was resting. A closer examination revealed that she had passed away overnight.

This was such a blow to Anthony and Theresa. Phyllis had developed health problems recently, but Dominic had been ill for quite a while. They were always worried that something might happen to Dominic due to his failing health, but no one was prepared for the loss of their mother. He thought Big John's visit might have had too much of an emotional impact on her. Anthony had to write to Johnny and break the bad news. The plan was to move the family to America before anything happened to Phyllis or Dominic. The plan was to unite everyone while their parents were still alive. With Phyllis gone, this was no longer possible.

Anthony made the funeral arrangements to bury his mother. He was unsure about what to write Johnny to inform him of their mother passing. He decided not to mention Big John's visit in the same letter. Maybe he would write about Big John's visit first, then several days later he would write of her passing. He did not want Johnny to know that she died the morning after Big John came to the house to discuss Johnny's life in the military. Anthony was not sure how to handle it.

He felt he was lucky to have his relationship with Anna. He had known her for several years and felt that they should take their relationship to the next level. After his mother's burial he would ask her to marry him. Anna knew of his hopes to move to America someday. In fact, she had relatives from Italy in Boston, Massachusetts.

"How far is Boston from New York?" Anthony would ask Johnny in his next letter. Perhaps it was time to really reunite as a family.

Chapter Eleven
Goodbye Mama

Johnny and Ray became close friends. Johnny would visit the gym on the nights Ray was working. He got to know Ralph the manager who was there on the night of his now-famous fight with Fred. The gym was usually closed at 9:00 PM and Johnny would help Ralph and Ray clean up.

Ralph asked Johnny if he wanted to earn some extra cash sparring with some of the customers.

"No, I am not a fighter," Johnny said.

"I can teach you and maybe you can fill in for me when I can't come in," Ray replied enthusiastically.

Johnny wasn't sure this was a good idea.

One night it was slow at the gym. Ray and Johnny were sitting around waiting for a customer to show up for a schedule sparring workout with Ray. The customer did not show up.

"Johnny, let's get into the ring and I will show you points on the sport of boxing."

"No Ray, I am done with fighting."

"Come on Johnny," Ray persisted. "We can pass the time and you may learn something."

Johnny felt obligated to Ray for all his help and friendship. In addition, Ray was still his supervisor at the mill. They went into the ring that night. It quickly became an ongoing training event consisting of regular boxing lessons for Johnny. Ray had boxed in the ring prior to working in the mill and left boxing for the steady paycheck that a regular job brought him. He was a sparring partner part time as well. It was less abusive than pursuing a boxing career at the age of forty. Boxing was a younger man's sport.

Several months later the gym announced that it was sponsoring an amateur boxing tournament. The winner would be awarded with a $50.00 cash prize. Ray told Johnny that he should sign up.

"Ray, I would like to win the $50.00, but I do not want to upset Mr. and Mrs. Pelosi again."

He told Ray how they reacted when he came home with his face swollen and a cut under his eye.

"Talk to them and tell them it will only be a couple of fights," said Ray. "I will be in your corner to stop the fight if I think you are overmatched."

"Johnny, I think you are ready. You learn fast." I think you will have a good chance to win the $50.00 with much less problems than your fight with Fred."

Johnny wanted to enter the contest, but he needed the approval of Mr. and Mrs. Pelosi first. This would not be easy. He would have to pick the right time to talk to them. He would approach Mr. Pelosi first. If he could convince him maybe they could both convince Mrs. Pelosi.

Meanwhile, back in Italy, the burial services for Phyllis were tiring and sad for Dominic, Anthony, and Theresa. There was a two-day wake for her in the farmhouse parlor room, a church ceremony, and then her burial in the Santoro family plot on the farm.

Several generations of Santoro's were buried there. The weather was cold and cloudy that day. After the burial, many friends and neighbors brought food and paid their respects with a visit to the farmhouse. Dominic was quiet and cordial, but his face was pale and drawn.

When all the visitors left, Anna and Theresa cleaned up and helped Dominic to bed. It was late, so Anna stayed over for the night. Both Anna and Theresa said goodnight to Anthony and turned in for the night.

Anthony stayed up late that evening and felt he had to write to Johnny before going to sleep. He sat alone and thought over carefully what he would write Johnny.

He chose his words carefully…

Dear Brother Johnny,

I am sad to write that our Mama has died. She had not been feeling well lately and passed away peacefully in her sleep. Many friends, relatives and neighbors have paid their respects. She was fortunate that one of your military comrades by the name of John Bonomo and his wife came to the farm house prior to her passing.

We invited them to dinner and enjoyed their company. He said you would remember him by the name of 'Big John.' The family was so impressed and happy with his stories on how brave you were serving under his command and during the terrible battle. He lost one leg as a result of the battle and was so pleased that you made it out safe and alive.

I have enclosed his address should you decide to write him. Johnny, as soon as Papa gets better, I will sell the farm. We will come to America and reunite our family. I plan to ask Anna to marry. She has relatives in Boston, Massachusetts in America. How far is Boston from where you live?

Love,
Brother Anthony

Anthony felt bad for Johnny. He would receive his letter with the terrible news of his mama's passing knowing that he could not return to Italy to attend the funeral or join the family in their sorrow. He hoped that Dominic's health would improve, but he did not feel optimistic that this would happen. He hoped that he would not have to write to Johnny again with even more sad news.

Johnny asked Mr. Pelosi if he could talk privately with him. Mr. Pelosi agreed. Johnny told him that he wanted to explain the circumstances of the fight with Fred. Everyone was so upset when Johnny came home with his face battered, he never was able to explain why he fought. He knew both Mr. and Mrs. Pelosi were disappointed in him and he must explain the events leading to the fight.

Mr. Pelosi listened.

Johnny went on to tell of the day when he was having his lunch and about the ethnic slurs that Fred had said. He told of Fred grabbing his sandwich and pushing him back and Ray his supervisor stepping in between them and breaking it up. Ray stopped a fight and possibly saved his job. He explained that Fred was upset because Johnny had replaced him on a job that he had and liked at the mill. Fred was sent to another department and he blamed Johnny. He was prejudiced against immigrants coming to this country to take jobs from American workers. Ray set up the fight at the gym knowing it would be safer for Johnny to have the fight supervised rather than Fred grabbing him alone some evening after work.

"I could not get out of fighting Fred one way or the other."

Johnny told Mr. Pelosi that Ray had helped him train the week before the fight and Johnny felt the only reason that he won was because of Ray's help.

"You won that fight?" Your face looked like you had lost!"

"Mrs. Pelosi and you did not give me a chance to tell you both what had happened," Johnny said with a sigh.

"What about this guy called Fred? Do you have to worry about future problems with him again?"

"No, he left the company and I have not seen him since. There is one more thing I would like to discuss with you."

"What is it?" Mr. Pelosi asked.

Johnny went on to tell Mr. Pelosi about the amateur boxing competition that the gym was running and that he would like to compete. Johnny had worked out with Ray and they both thought that Johnny would do well. Each bout would consist of only three rounds, each three minutes long, with one-minute rest in between.

Ray would be in Johnny's corner and would stop the fight if Johnny did not do as well as they expected him to do. Ray knew all the amateur boxers that worked out of the gym that would sign up and he thought Johnny had a very good chance to win.

"I understand how you feel Johnny. It is good for you to learn how to take care of yourself. But, if you end up being hurt or come home battered like you did after your fight with Fred, Rose would never forgive either one of us. Allow me to think it over. I would also like to meet your friend Ray and discuss it with him."

Johnny felt relieved that he was able to explain to Mr. Pelosi why he was involved in the fight with Fred. He called Ray and asked him if he would meet with Mr. Pelosi and Ray agreed. Johnny and Mr. Pelosi dropped by the gym the following evening. Ray was in the ring sparring with one of the fighters when they arrived. They both watched Ray until he was finished. Johnny introduced Ray to Mr. Pelosi.

"You seem to be very familiar with the sport of boxing," said Mr. Pelosi to Ray.

"I did box in my younger days for many years. It is a sport for the young. My days are done," Ray said. "I still love to get into the ring, but I am no longer able to compete at my age, so I help train and work out with the younger folk."

"You must think that Johnny has a talent for it. Johnny told me that both of you think he would do well in this upcoming boxing tournament."

"I do. Most of the applicants all work out of this gym and I know their capability. They are all amateurs with little experience in the boxing ring. Johnny told me he will not sign up for the tournament without the blessing of Mrs. Pelosi and you. I would be in Johnny's corner and would do my best to be very watchful to make sure that Johnny does not get hurt."

"I have to think this over and I have to think of a way to convince my wife to go along with it. Johnny told me why he had to fight that guy Fred and I want to thank you for stepping in and setting it up supervised in the ring rather than it happening in a street fight somewhere. We did not give Johnny a chance to explain any of the circumstances leading up to the fight."

Carmen talked with Rose and convinced her that they should allow Johnny to experiment with boxing as long as he is supervised by his friend Ray. Rose did not want to watch Johnny in the ring and hoped that this was the right thing to do. Johnny signed up for the tournament using Johnny Saint Gold for his boxing name. He felt it would bring him some luck. Ray agreed. His first three round fight was scheduled in three weeks on a Saturday morning. All the bouts would be scheduled on the weekends to allow the participants the ability to work at their primary jobs during the weekdays. Ray developed a workout program and schedule for Johnny after work each evening at the gym, and a jog each morning before work. All Johnny could think of was the tournament. He trained hard. He trained to win.

Chapter Twelve
Amateur Boxing

The week before the tournament Johnny received a letter from his brother Anthony informing him his mother had passed away. Johnny was shocked. He knew his father was ill, but he never expected he would lose his mother. He felt very sad at first, and then very angry. He felt life had cheated him and his family. They had been through so much. He would never see his mother again. He never had the opportunity to say goodbye to her.

Ray asked him if he wanted to pull out of the tournament.

"No," said Johnny, now more determined than ever to win.

He became very quiet and worked out very hard. He could not think about anything else except for the loss of his mother. He ran so fast and far before work in the morning that he was drenched with sweat. He would hit the punching bag so hard in the gym that onlookers could not take their eyes off him.

On the first day of the tournament Johnny showed up early. Carmen came alone to watch Johnny. Rose did not want to watch the fight.

Carmen asked Johnny. "Are you all right?"

"I am fine," Johnny said, leaving little doubt that he was ready.

Ray greeted Carmen and shook his hand and said to Johnny. "Let's get ready to go in the ring."

Shortly afterwards, Johnny and his opponent stepped into the ring. The gym was packed with relatives and friends of the fighters. A gentleman talked to the two fighters and round one started. Johnny and his opponent both threw punches which did not land initially. His opponent had some restraint and did not swing wildly like Fred. Johnny still had his mother in his thoughts and took a punch in the nose. Blood spurted out and his nose hurt at first, and then went numb. He got very angry and thought to himself, "I cannot go home battered up again. "Mrs. Pelosi will be furious at me and Mr. Pelosi."

He became very aggressive and threw combinations to his opponent's head and midsection while trying to protect his face from other blows. He pushed his opponent into the ropes, saw an opening and threw an uppercut hard to his opponent's chin. His opponent went down fast and did not get up. He was knocked out. Johnny could not believe what he did. It was fast. He went back to his corner.

"Where did you get that punch?" Ray asked in amazement.

When Ray and Johnny would train and spar with each other they both pulled their punches. Ray had no idea Johnny had a powerful knockout punch. All fighters hit the punching bag hard in training but a knockout win in the first round was not something that many fighters could accomplish.

Mr. Pelosi came over and proudly shook Johnny's hand. "Put some ice on that nose before you come home," he said, almost affectionately.

Carmen went home right after the fight and told Rose that Johnny was impressive, and she would be proud of him. Rose still did not like the idea of fighting and hoped that this was something Johnny had to get out of his system.

Ray told Johnny that he knew and sparred with his first opponent. "It was a good win. The next fight would be the next week. Now that we know you have a serious weapon, we will work on your right hand and develop ways to deliver it."

The next week, Johnny continued to work hard training. Ray and Johnny became very close friends and they were seen together at the gym practically every evening.

The next fight went longer than Johnny's first one. Before the end of the third round Johnny scored another knockout again. The next match was scheduled for the following Saturday. All the other boxers were now concerned with the effectiveness of Johnny's right hand. Johnny was developing a reputation that put fear into the other boxers.

On Monday morning Rose had prepared Johnny's lunch for his workday at the mill and handed it to him, but she had a question that had been bothering her.

"Do you really want to become a boxer for your primary occupation?" Rose asked Johnny.

Johnny thought about it carefully before he answered. "No, I don't. I have to admit that I love to win, but I am not foolish enough to think that I could make a steady living boxing. Plus, in this tournament, all the fighters are part time amateurs like me. Please don't worry. I am having fun and keeping myself in shape at the same time."

"When you get through with this tournament, I would like you to leave the mill and come back and work for Carmen. Maybe he can afford to pay you more now that his business has picked up."

"We will see."

Rose looked lovingly at Johnny. "I love you Johnny. You're the son I never had. I don't want you to be hurt anymore."

"I love you too mama."

Johnny had never called Rose mama before this, although she was like a mother to him since the first day they met. It seemed normal all of a sudden to call her mama, especially after the loss of his real mother in Italy. He thought to himself, "With all the sadness that I have had, I am also very lucky for the blessings I have. To be accepted into the Pelosi family is truly a great blessing." They hugged each other. Rose cried after Johnny left for work. She always loved him like the son they never had.

Chapter Thirteen

Letters

A letter from Angelo to Johnny…

Dear Johnny,

I am sorry to hear from your brother Anthony that you lost your mother. I will pray for her. I also lost both my mother and farther since our trip to America. Anthony and I have communicated by mail with each other since I first wrote to your family and he has kept me up to date on your activities in our new country. Anthony told me he will marry and come to America with the family in the near future. I like your brother and hope to meet Anthony and your family when they arrive. I of course want to see you again. Hopefully we can all get together.

I am not far from you. I live and work in New York City and maybe we could meet with each other before your reunion with your brother if his trip to America is delayed. I have a well-paying job and work for a very influential Italian family. I met a nice girl and we are very happy together. Perhaps I could get you a job with the family. I already mentioned you to my boss as my buddy Johnny Saint Gold, and I think there will be no problem if you want to move and work in the big city. We will discuss it further when we meet. Anthony informed me that Frank and Nick are doing well in Spain and Nick has opened his own bakery. I am glad we all survived. Meanwhile, I have enclosed my address should you want to write me.

Sincerely,
Your friend, Angelo

Johnny was glad to hear from Angelo and wanted to sit down and write back to him. He was so busy now with all his boxing activity he would have to put it off. He recently wrote to Big John to thank him for his visit to his family.

A letter from Johnny to Big John…

Dear Big John,
I want to thank you for visiting my family with your wife. They were so pleased to meet and talk with you. I thank you for all the nice things you said to them about me. I am so sorry that you lost your leg in the battle. You were my protector and I will never forget what you did for me. I am forever in your debt. I hope someday we will meet to discuss our experiences. Have you ever thought of coming to the new country? There is plenty of work available, good pay and a freedom to pursue whatever you choose to do.

Sincerely,
Johnny Santoro

Chapter Fourteen
Dearest Rose

Johnny and Ray practiced on the delivery of Johnny's right hand punch. They worked out various combinations that were successful for the next two fights. Johnny won both fights achieved by another knockout in the third round and the other by a decision. The next fight would be the tournament semi- finals.

New York Hospital

The day before the fight Johnny came home from the mill after work to have a fast dinner and go back to the gym to practice with Ray. No one was home, which was very unusual. The Pelosi family always sat down together for the evening meal.

A note was left on the table for Johnny. "Johnny, mom is ill. Had to rush her to the hospital"

He went to the hospital and found Carmen, Donna, and Lucy in the waiting room.

"Is mom all right?"

"We really don't know. The girls and I are waiting to speak to the doctor who is with her now. She had terrible pains in her right side. The pains started two days ago. She thought the pains would go away but they didn't. She refused to see a doctor or go to the hospital until the pain got so bad that she could not stand it."

The doctor came in the room and approached the family.

"Rose is very ill, and her illness is diagnosed as appendicitis. Her appendix is inflamed and could burst causing a fluid to infect her abdominal cavity," the doctor said, clearly concerned. "This condition could be fatal if not treated immediately."

"How do you treat it?" asked Carmen.

The doctor chose his words carefully. "I'll need to operate and remove the appendix as soon as possible."

"Doctor, what are her chances for survival if you operate now?" By now, Carmen was close to panic, the very thought of losing his beloved Rose unfathomable.

"I don't know until I operate."

Silence filled the room.

It was Carmen who spoke. "Do it!"

Rose did not want to be operated on. She was scared. Carmen, Johnny, and the girls tried to convince her that this was the only thing to do. The operation would be done as soon as the doctor could set it up that evening.

Rose said to Johnny. "Go home and rest. You have your semifinal fight tomorrow. I do not want you hurt."

"No, I am not leaving until I know you are going to be well," Johnny said firmly.

"Johnny please," Rose implored. "I will be so worried if you're not in shape before the fight due to my illness. Go home and get some rest. I will be fine."

"I do not want you to worry about me. I am not going to fight tomorrow. I am going to stay here with you and our family. You are more important than any fight."

The family waited for the operation to be completed. The doctor promised to report to them the results as soon as he finished. Everyone sat still without much conversation. Hours passed, and everyone watched the door they expected the doctor to enter. Johnny was worried, as was the rest of the family.

He prayed in silence, "Dear God, please allow her to survive. I already lost one mother. Please allow her to pull through this operation."

It was very late, and everyone had spread out on the sofas in the waiting room. They were all very tired and the girls had closed their eyes, but no one could go to sleep.

The doctor came through the door and everyone sprang to their feet.

He told them that while he was successful in removing the appendix, it burst open and some of the fluid had spilled out in her abdomen. They tried to remove the fluid but had no assurances that an infection would not occur. He would have preferred to have removed the appendix intact before it burst.

Carmen asked. "Doctor, will she be okay?"

The doctor replied, "I truly don't know. We have to wait and hope that the spilled fluid causes no problems."

"How long until we know?" Weary and worried, Carmen didn't want to miss anything.

"Every case is different. She will have to stay in the hospital until we are sure that she has completely recovered and that she has no sign of any infection. There will be an around the clock vigil by the hospital staff and I will check in with her in the morning."

"When can we see her?" This time it was Johnny asking. Like Carmen, the very thought of losing Rose was unthinkable.

"Not now. We will talk again in the morning after I see her. I am sure the nursing staff will keep you updated if there is any change in her condition."

The doctor left, and Carmen turned to Johnny and the girls and said, "The three of you go home, rest and have breakfast. I will stay and sleep on one of the sofas here in the hospital."

They all complained that they should stay also.

"Please go home and come back in the morning. Go home! I want you all to listen to your father. I will see you after you rest and have breakfast."

Johnny and the girls reluctantly left Carmen alone in the hospital. Carmen sat down and tried to relax but he couldn't.

He thought of what he would do if he ever lost Rose. She was still his beautiful bride. In his eyes she had not aged at all. Her beautiful big brown eyes and long black silky hair was sometimes tied up in a bun. She was a pleasant soft-spoken person, a good listener, wonderful mother, and trusted partner. She was unselfish. They never had any arguments or real disagreement. When there was a problem, they would sit down and discuss it rationally. They worked things out together. Carmen needed her. He loved her. And now he risked losing her.

The words *"Till death do us part"* went over and over again in his mind.

The years had flown by too quickly. They deserved more time together. He closed his eyes and prayed like he never prayed before. He remembered so many happy events over the years that he had spent with Rose. He remembered the births of his two daughters. He thought of the day that Rose and he met Johnny on the opposite side of the fence at the seaport terminal. Johnny looked so scared and helpless and pleaded with them to help, first with tears in his eyes and then breaking down and crying. Rose and Carmen stepped away from the fence to discuss what to do. It felt like just yesterday. It was as if Johnny had always been a part of his family.

He remembered what Rose said.

"Carmen, we must help this boy. I think it is fate that brought the three of us together. I keep thinking this was meant to be as retribution to our loss of our son at birth. Please tell him to climb over the fence."

Johnny had truly filled the position of a son to both Rose and Carmen. He prayed all night for Rose's recovery.

Early the next day a nurse came out to talk to Carmen.

"Your wife is very ill and only time will reveal if she will pull through. The doctor will be in later this morning to talk with you. You have time to go home and rest if you want. Recovery for procedures such as your wife had will take a while."

"Thank you, I will wait to see the doctor as soon as I can, and I would appreciate any updates on my wife that you can give me while I wait for the doctor."

Johnny, Donna, and Lucy returned with food and coffee for Carmen. They had many questions for him that he could not answer. He explained to them that they would all have to wait for the doctor's report.

The clock ticked away slowly. It was noontime before the doctor came into the waiting area to see the family to report on Rose's post-operative exam. He told them she was very ill and still in great danger, and the family could see her but only for a very short stay. They would allow only two visitors at a time.

Carmen and his older daughter Lucy would go in first, and when they came out Johnny and Donna would be allowed to see Rose.

Rose looked pale and her face appeared very drawn. Her voice was very weak, and it was hard for her to keep her eyes open. They did not stay with her long to comply with the doctor's instructions. They all remained in the waiting area until late afternoon when Carmen asked the nurse if they could visit her again for a short visit. She looked more tired during the second visit. Carmen told everyone to go home and have dinner. He would stay in the hospital overnight again in the waiting room. Such was the strength of his love for her that he was unable to leave.

It was Sunday morning. Johnny, Lucy, and Donna went to an early church service. They all had trouble sleeping the night before. When they came home from church, Ray dropped in to visit Johnny. Ray did not know why Johnny did not show up for the match, but he thought it must have been something important for Johnny to default his standing in the tournament. Ray was understanding after learning of Rose's health. He told Johnny there would be other opportunities to fight again and that he would pray for Rose's recovery. Johnny could only think of Rose and that he must support Carmen in his diligence to care for Rose and the family.

Johnny and the girls returned to the hospital and brought food for Carmen after Ray left their house. Carmen looked tired and there was no change in Rose's condition. They all had the opportunity again to visit Rose and reluctantly left after Carmen insisted that they go home and told Johnny to go to work the next morning. Johnny was concerned with how Rose looked but did not mention it to Carmen and the girls. He suspected that they were all as concerned as he was.

Johnny went to work the next day and was looking forward to visiting Rose that evening. When he arrived home, there was a letter for him from Angelo. He was excited to open it. He had his mind continually on Rose since the start of her illness and looked forward to reading what Angelo had to say.

Angelo wrote:

Dear Johnny,

I did not receive a reply to the letter I sent. I hope you received it. I know you are probably busy, but I would like to meet you to go over old times and catch up on what you are doing now. I am doing well, and I have received several promotions and have workers under my supervision. Perhaps you can visit me some weekend. You can stay in my apartment and I can show you around the Big Apple, as they call it. I regret the commotion of us separating when we got off the boat, but it eventually worked out for both of us. Your brother Anthony wrote that you are happy and settled in with your foster family. I hope this letter finds you well. Please reply so I know you are getting my mail.

Sincerely,
Your friend, Angelo

Johnny felt embarrassed that he did not reply to Angelo's first letter. He meant to but did not find writing letters easy when he was so busy. He went to see Rose and stayed a short while. She was about the same. The doctor said recovery would be slow. When he returned home, he sat down and wrote to Angelo.

Dear Angelo,

I am sorry I did not promptly answer your first letter. My foster mother is very ill recovering from an operation in the hospital. As soon as everything settles down, I will write to you again and make plans to visit you. It will have to be on a weekend, so I do not have to miss work. I am glad things are going well for you. I have a friend named Ray and wonder if I could take him with me to meet you. He is a very nice guy and I know you would like him. He is my supervisor at the mill and has previous boxing experience. Ray has helped me train to compete in an amateur boxing tournament. I did well but had to withdraw in the semi-finals due to the sudden illness of my foster mother.

Sincerely,
Your friend Johnny

Johnny was old enough to decide to visit Angelo without the permission of Mr. And Mrs. Pelosi but thought it would be better to have Ray accompany him on the trip when he broached the subject to them.

Several weeks passed and Rose returned home from the hospital. She was still very weak. The doctor said it would take time for her to fully recover. Johnny received a letter from Anthony that his father had passed away.

Anthony wrote:

My Dear Brother Johnny,

I am sorry to tell you that Papa passed peacefully in his sleep. It was expected but still a shock when it happened. Just the other night he talked about meeting our beloved mother soon and said some day we would all meet up in the afterlife with Mama and Papa. I am sure that will be so. After a period of mourning for Pa's passing, I plan to marry Anna and try to sell the farm. We will come to America. As I mentioned in previous letters, Anna has family in Boston, Massachusetts. They told me that they have a job waiting for me. Johnny, we will finally see each other again. I have asked our sister Theresa to come with us. Our family will reunite in the new world. I will write again and update you when we are ready to leave for America.

Love,
Brother Anthony

Johnny sat down and again had thoughts of his home and family in Italy. It was sad to believe he would never see his Mama and Papa again. He would have loved to say goodbye to them. It was so long since he had seen them. Sometimes he had to concentrate to remember their expressions when they laughed. Life had been both good and bad for Johnny. He looked forward to the future and of seeing his brother and sister again.

Johnny thought he would enjoy seeing Angelo, so he asked Ray the next day if he wanted to go to New York to meet with Angelo over a weekend. Ray said yes. Johnny told Rose and Carmen that he would like to visit with Angelo with Ray. They would make the trip on a Saturday and Sunday, so as not to miss work. Rose and Carmen were relieved that Ray would accompany him. They would always worry about Johnny.

Chapter Fifteen
The Big Apple

Several weeks later Johnny and Ray traveled to New York City to meet Angelo. He was very pleased to see Johnny and happy to meet Ray. He lived in a lavish apartment with his girlfriend Lori. Angelo dressed well and appeared to be living a very good life.

"Johnny, you have grown into a strong and handsome man and you look well. Tell me about your job and what you both do for a living," Angelo said, clearly happy to see his old friend.

"My job is nothing important. I work in a mill as a laborer and Ray is my good friend and supervisor. He also has taught me the art of boxing. Ray was a boxer and he is a sparring partner for some of the boxers in our local gym." said Johnny. "I did well in a local amateur tournament, but I had to default the semi-final match due to my foster mother's illness. I can see you have done well. I thought when I lost you in the ship terminal that I would never see you again."

Angelo thought back to that fated day so long ago.

"Johnny, I am so sorry we got separated. When I helped to unload a package from the boat to the loading dock with Nino, I tried to escape under the rope. I must have caught the inspector's eye. He shouted to me to stop. I ran, and he chased me. I did not go left at the fence as we were instructed to do by

Nino. I knew you had gone left, and I did not want them to catch you, so I turned right."

Johnny felt humbled that Angelo would do this for him in an effort to help Johnny to be able to escape capture.

"I ran into a couple of other inspectors and after a short struggle, I was apprehended. They took me to a room and wanted to know how I arrived and who had helped me. I said nothing in an effort to protect Nino. They eventually put me in another room with a single guard. I jumped him and got away. Before we docked, Nino gave me an address of a friend for us to contact when we arrived in the city. I found my way there and he helped me get a job. I worked hard to prove myself and now I make lots of money. I am in a position to help both of you."

"What type of help?" Johnny asked. The thought of making more money and leaving the mill had an appeal to him.

"I can give you both good jobs making plenty of money. You would work directly for me. I would have to vouch for you with my boss in the family I work for but that should not be a problem. I am a good producer. They trust and like me. The family I work for came from Sicily and watches over the Italian neighborhood in New York City. There are other areas of New York City that have organizations in charge such as the one in the Irish neighborhood."

Angelo was speaking of things unfamiliar to Johnny and Ray, but by now, he had their attention.

"Our family looks out for the Italian immigrants that come over from Italy and settle in New York.

Like a bank, we loan money. People who cannot borrow from a bank because of a lack of collateral can borrow money from our family. One of my jobs is to make sure our borrowers pay it back. If loans are not paid back to a bank it will go out of business. It is the same with the loans we give. The money must be paid back, or the family will not be able to loan money again to people

Early 1900's New York City

who need it. We also collect a surcharge from the businesses in our jurisdiction to protect them from outsiders interfering in their business. It is a form of insurance. There are other activities that we are involved in. But first, let me show you around."

Angelo took Johnny and Ray for a tour of the Italian area within the city of New York. They visited restaurants, clubs, dance halls, and private casinos. Everywhere they went everyone warmly greeted Angelo with respect. Lori was beautiful. They were a very classy couple.

Johnny and Ray were treated like royalty and this was a visit they both thoroughly enjoyed. The weekend flew by and it was time to say goodbye.

"Johnny, I am so glad to see you again. Ray, it was a pleasure meeting you. Think over my offer and hopefully we will all see each other again soon."

"Thank you for your great hospitality. We will think over your offer and get back to you. I have one question for you before I leave that I have thought about often. Where did you get all that money that you carried in the bag that financed our trip to America?"

Angelo smiled. "From the Italian army of course. They brought Italian lira and local currencies to Africa to pay the troops in cash. It was stored in a safe in the regimental supply wagon and I relieved it from them after the battle at Adwa when we decided to leave. It was small payment for the trouble they caused us. Johnny, I told you I was a banker."

There was a bit of a mischievous sparkle in his eyes as he spoke. Both Johnny and Ray wondered if there might be more to Angelo's business dealings than he was letting on.

Johnny and Ray returned home with a lot to think about. Ray was very impressed with Angelo and told Johnny that this is a once-in-a-lifetime opportunity for both of them. Ray's father and mother migrated to Canada from Italy. Ray was born in Canada and was not as familiar with the backgrounds of the powerful families of Sicily.

Johnny remembered his father Dominic telling him stories of the vendettas and the influence these families had over the people in southern Italy. They were called "The Mafia." The family members took an oath to obey a code of loyalty and silence called the Omerta. In America they were called "La Cosa Nostra."

Ray was seriously considering accepting Angelo's offer. He was getting older and saw no future financial reward at the mill compared to what Angelo offered.

"I am glad I had the chance to visit Angelo, but I am not going to accept his offer. I owe him so much for his help and guidance from the time I met him in the desert to the time we got off the ship in America, but I do not want to get involved in what I believe may be illegal work. My brother and sister will be coming to America and it is too soon for me to think about any job changes."

Ray considered Johnny's words before he replied. "At my age, I will never earn enough money with my current jobs. I can earn more with your friend Angelo. Thank you for introducing me to him and I only hope that you will not be upset if I accept his offer. I want us to remain friends and I understand the risk that I may be taking. If it is okay with you, I am going to work for Angelo. I think he is a nice guy and I do not think it will be as risky as you believe it to be.'

"Ray, we will always be friends and I wish you the best of luck. Keep in touch."

Ray went off to the big city and Johnny missed seeing him at work. It was not the same. It was an adjustment having a new supervisor at the mill who was not his close friend. It also was not as much fun at the gym without Ray.

Chapter Sixteen
Flee or Die

Johnny had so much on his mind with the likely trip of Anthony and his sister coming to America in the near future. His brother Anthony was planning to go to Boston, Massachusetts with his new wife Anna and his sister Theresa. Johnny never informed Anthony how far Massachusetts was from New York. He wished it was closer. Johnny knew Anna would want to be close to her relatives.

He wanted to see his brother and sister again. He needed to talk to someone to discuss his thoughts and hopes for his future. Johnny wondered if he should move to Boston to reunite with his brother and sister.

He needed to talk to Rose and Carmen. This would be difficult. Rose was still not well. It had to be Carmen. Rose's health was not improving as the doctor's claimed it would. She was still very weak. Carmen and Rose were his adoptive family and had done so much for him.

Johnny was torn between his brother and sister and Carmen and Rose. He thought he should not talk to Carmen until after Anthony and Theresa arrive and got settled in Boston. Anthony said he could get him a job with his wife Anna's relatives who had settled in Boston several years ago. He decided to see what developed. He had a good job at the mill. He could make a trip to visit them after they arrive to see what kind of job would be available for him in Boston. Johnny needed to calm down and relax. Too many things had happened lately. He didn't want to make a rash decision or upset Carmen and Rose until he had more facts.

Several months passed and Johnny was leaving work for the day when he was greeted by Ray just outside the mill entry. He was pleased to see Ray and greeted him with a hug.

"Ray, I am so happy to see you. What are you doing here? Is everything okay?"

Ray looked pale and frightened. "No Johnny, everything is not okay. Not even close."

"What's wrong?" Johnny sensed that Ray was afraid.

"They killed him," Ray said, his eyes darting about.

"They killed who? What are you talking about?"

"They killed Angelo!" By now, Ray was in a full-on panic.

Johnny was stunned to learn about the death of his lifelong friend. "Oh my God! I can't believe that. Who killed him and why? What happened?"

Ray went on to explain, "They broke into their apartment and shot both Angelo and Lori. Angelo told me that no one except the head of the family and you and I knew where he lived. He made me take an oath that I would not tell anyone. The family knew that we stayed in his apartment for the weekend we visited Angelo. They did not know who you are except for your nickname Johnny Saint Gold. They don't know where you live but they know me. They call my position a soldier and one of the other soldiers who worked with me in Angelo's group asked me some questions the day after the murder that made me feel uncomfortable."

"What kind of questions?" Johnny was getting more uneasy by the moment.

"Where did I live before I joined Angelo's group? Who you are and where do you live?" I told him nothing. We were interrupted, and I was able to get out of continuing the conversation. But I know they think that we were involved. I packed my things and left which makes it look even worse. I could not take a chance to stay for another interrogation or possible retaliation. Johnny, you were right. They are a bad group to mess with. I am sorry that I did not listen to your warning."

It took a moment for it all to sink in. "Ray, now I am worried for the both of us. Angelo may have told them where we live."

"I don't think so. From what I learned during my employment, they move fast. I think they would have been here now if they knew where you lived. They would have never asked me any questions about you." Ray continued, "I think we will both be okay if they do not catch me and I do not intend to let them do so. I have family in Canada and I am going to leave tonight. I just came by to tell you what happened to Angelo. I am sorry that I did not follow your advice. I will not write you or do anything that would jeopardize your safety. I hope we will someday see each other again."

Ray left, and Johnny could not get Angelo's death and Ray's concern out of his mind. He planned to discuss this with Carmen. He did not want to put the Pelosi family in any danger. As soon as he arrived home from work that night he asked where Carmen was. Carmen would be home late. He was having dinner with a client. Johnny would wait to see Carmen. He did not want to mention anything about his problem to Rose. She was very tired and went to bed shortly after dinner.

Johnny thought to himself, "Why do these things happen to me?" He realized that life is strange, and events happen beyond your control. He remembered being kidnapped by the Italian militia and all the good and bad events that followed. All these events were beyond his control. Your life events, both good or bad, are created by each of the people that cross your path during your journey. You have to make the best of it. This thing with Angelo. What could I have done differently that would have protected me from being involved with this terrible event? They are searching for me now. It happened, and I will have to deal with it.

Carmen came home, and they sat down and talked. Johnny went over all the events, his discussion with Ray, and his concern for the safety of Ray, himself, and the Pelosi family. Carmen agreed that Ray's decision to leave for Canada was probably the right thing to do. He also thought that if the New York family knew where Johnny was, they would have made contact by now.

"Should I leave home to protect our family?" Johnny asked, unsure as to his next step.

"I don't think so. I cannot say that I am not worried, but I don't think there is anything we can do about it. I think Ray is correct if they knew who you are and where you live they would have been here by now."

Carmen looked tired and was still very worried about Rose's health.

"Johnny, this is not your fault. Let's pray that everything will be fine."

Chapter Seventeen
Goodbye Sweet Rose

Weeks passed, and Johnny and Carmen said nothing more about the Angelo affair. Rose's health had not improved, and the family was preoccupied with Rose's constant visits to the doctor and their hope that she would ultimately get well.

Anthony had sold the farm in Italy and had finally arrived in Boston, Massachusetts with his Wife Anna and sister Theresa. The three of them moved into an apartment on Hanover Street in The North End neighborhood of Boston, in the heart of the Italian district. They lived not far from Anna's cousins who owned a meat business called Boston Provisions on Blackstone Street. Anthony went to work for their company. Theresa and Anna got jobs with a pasta manufacturing company located on Prince Street, also not far from their apartment.

Rose was not feeling well and had gone into the hospital again. Johnny decided to wait until she was released and returned home before he made the trip to Boston. Sadly, he did not have to wait long.

Johnny, Carmen, Lucy, and Donna spent most of their available time visiting Rose hoping for her recovery, but it was not meant to be. Late one evening Rose passed. She was laid to rest. It was a tremendous loss for the entire Pelosi family, and especially for Johnny.

He thought about all the family and friends that had passed since the start of his journey when he was forced to leave home with the militia. His losses were many. He had lost his mother Phyllis, his father Dominic, his adopted mother Rose, his friend Angelo. He would never see any of them again in this world.

Everyone in the Pelosi family seemed to change without their beloved Rose. Life at home seemed so silent. Conversations at dinner were minimized. The sound of the clock in the dining room could be heard for the first time. Everyone tried to fill in some of the void Rose's loss had caused.

The girls took over all the cooking and house cleaning activities. Carmen visited her gravesite early every morning. Life continued for the Pelosi family, but it was not the same.

Several months later, Johnny left to finally meet with his brother and sister in Boston. When he arrived, he was surprised to see that Boston's North End was very similar to the Italian District in New York City. It had a lot of activity. There were push cart peddlers everywhere and small restaurants and cafes on every corner.

The streets were busy with pedestrians, horse-driven carriages and automobile traffic all mixed together in a chaotic rhythm. The large population was enough to support the North Meeting House church and the North Burying Ground. Early grave markers in the cemetery showed dates as early as 1661. Older wooden buildings were being replaced by four-to-five story brick apartment buildings. The neighborhood was being revitalized.

The reunion between Johnny, his brother and sister was many years overdue. It was emotional and happy. There were lots of hugs, tears and smiles. Anthony and Theresa were shocked of the transformation of their brother Johnny from a young lad to a tall well-built handsome adult man with black hair and piercing brown eyes. Anthony had not changed much. He looked somewhat like he did when Johnny was kidnapped by the militia, only an older version, with a bit of receding hair. Theresa was petite and beautiful with light skin and dark hair. Anthony's wife Anna was pretty, had a nice smile and very pleasant. They ate, drank and toasted to their reunion.

The next day Anthony and Johnny visited Anthony's place of work. Anthony introduced Johnny to his employers who happened to be Anna's cousins. They discussed employment possibilities for Johnny. He was offered a job at the meat packing plant as an apprentice meat cutter similar to the position that Anthony had. It was hard work but very good pay. After a six-month training it would lead to a position as a meat cutter with the ability to break down the complete carcass of beef or lamb into steaks, roasts, etc. It was a blue-collar trade in big demand in Boston.

Johnny thanked them for the job offer but needed time to think it over. He was told that the offer would be there waiting for him should he ever decide to move to Boston in the future. Anthony told Johnny that if he accepted the position and they both learned their trade well they could eventually go into their own retail business as partners. It certainly was something to think about. It was time for Johnny to return to the Pelosi household. Johnny was thankful to see his family in Boston and promised to visit them again soon.

Johnny returned home and was greeted by Carmen, Lucy, and Donna. They all wanted to know how the visit went with his brother and sister and what Boston was like. They talked for hours and told Johnny just how much he was missed. Carmen was not the same as he was when Rose was alive.

Johnny thought to himself, "When you lose a loved one a little bit of yourself dies with them." He knew from experience how he felt when he lost both of his mothers, his father Dominic, and even his friend Angelo.

He did not tell them about the job offer made to him and of his thoughts of moving to Boston to reunite with his brother and sister. It was not the time to discuss these things with the Pelosi family. He needed to think about whether or not he should leave the Pelosi family for Boston. They had done so much for him and he loved them. Carmen and the girls needed him. He needed more time. How could he ever leave them?

The next day Johnny went to work at the mill, but his mind was not on his job. He thought of Boston and of what an exciting place it was. It was great to see his brother and sister again. It would have been complete if his mother Louise and his father Dominic had lived and come to America as was planned.

Carmen had a phone installed in their home and Anthony could be reached by phone in Boston.

Johnny would call Anthony by phone very occasionally with the excuse of the high cost of making the call to Boston. The real reason was that Anthony would always pursue the discussions on Johnny's move to Boston. Johnny did not want to talk about it. He was caught in the middle of both families. He would frequent the gym after work as an excuse not to be home when Anthony called. He decided he would have to explain to Anthony that he would move to Boston to join them someday, but now was not the best time while the Pelosi family was still in mourning for Rose. He placed their needs above his own.

Chapter Eighteen
Welcome to the Suburbs

That night he went to the gym to work out. Ralph the manager approached him and told him that he had a visit from two strangers. They asked questions about Ray and his friend Johnny Saint Gold. Ralph told them that Ray had worked there and left to take a job in the city and he had not seen him since. The strangers said they were friends of both Ray and Johnny, but Ralph got suspicious when they asked for Johnny Saint Gold's last name and where he lived. Ralph told him he did not know Johnny's last name or where he lived. They asked him if he had seen him lately. Ralph was very uncomfortable with their questions and told them he had not seen either Ray or Johnny since Ray quit his job at the gym. He warned Johnny to be careful. Ralph told Johnny he was glad he did not know his address.

Johnny felt a cold sweat come over him. He was fortunate that Ralph did not know his address and they apparently did not know his last name. He would have to stay away from the gym. As far as he knew, no one else at the gym knew his address or his last name. Everyone at the gym called him Johnny Saint Gold. Only Ray knew who he was or where he lived. Hopefully Ray was still safe and alive in Canada.

Johnny asked Carmen if they could sit down and talk after dinner about the conversation that he had with Ralph relative to the two visitors. Carmen listened carefully without interrupting Johnny. He was visibly concerned.

After a few moments of silence, Carmen responded, "Johnny, I want you to stay away from the gym for good. They seem to be relentless in their search for both Ray and you. I worry not only for your safety but the safety of your two sisters Lucy and Donna. If these men find out where you live, there will be trouble for us all."

"I understand. I do not want to put our family in any danger. Maybe I should put some space between myself and the family for a while. I could go to Boston and work with my brother. What do you think about that?"

Carmen considered Johnny's offer. "I hate to have you leave us, but it may not be a bad idea for a while. It is up to you Johnny, but if you decide to go to Boston, you must not tell anyone where you're going, even your sisters. When you give your notice at work, tell them you are going to work in another country. Make it difficult for anyone to track you."

Johnny quickly called his brother Anthony and told him he would accept the job offer as a meat cutter apprentice and arrive in Boston as soon as he could make arrangements to do so. He went into work the next day and told his supervisor he had to leave his job without giving a notice due to personal reasons. He told them he had family in Australia that needed him to help run the family farm due to health problems. He had always been a good productive worker at the mill and they were agreeable to pay him his wages due when he left that day. It was happening so fast, Johnny did not have much time to dwell on what he was doing.

Johnny arrived on a Saturday morning and was greeted by his brother Anthony and his sister Theresa. They had made accommodations for Johnny to live in

their home in Boston. He had planned to live alone within a close distance but separate from his Boston family. He thought it would protect them from the possibility of a

Bustling Boston Neighborhood

visit from the New York people who had questioned Ralph about Johnny Saint Gold. Johnny felt they would all be safe in Boston, but why take any chances. He would look for a separate apartment after he started his new job and settled in but did not say anything to them about his plans for now. They celebrated their reunion and enjoyed the weekend together.

Monday morning started a new life experience for Johnny. He started his new job as an apprentice at the meat distributer. Although he went to work with his brother Anthony, they did not work together or see each other until lunch or quitting time. Anthony had completed his training as an apprentice and worked in the retail department while Johnny started his training in another department with several other trainees. He worked and trained side-by-side with another trainee named Joseph DeGiammerino.

Joseph's nickname was Joey D. He was very friendly, and Johnny and Joey hit it off right away. Joey rented an apartment north of Boston in a suburb named Malden. Their friendship grew each day. Johnny told him he would like to have his own apartment and Joey immediately asked him if he wanted to move in with him. The rent was reasonable. If they both shared tenancy it would allow both of them to save money. Johnny told him he would think about it.

The next weekend Johnny went to see where Joey lived. His apartment was in a section of Malden called Edgeworth. Malden had a mix of immigrants from many countries, though predominately Irish, Italian and Jewish. Joey's apartment was located in the center of several blocks of two-family homes owned or rented by Italian residents. There was a small dairy with approximately fifty milking cows where fresh milk could be purchased or set up for home delivery. Most of the homes had vegetable gardens in the back yards. The dairy sold buckets of cow dung to the residents for their gardens. Johnny loved the neighborhood.

Although it was not as country as his farm in Italy, it was not as busy as Boston. He could feel comfortable there. He told Joey he would move in with him.

When Anthony was told of Johnny's plan to move, he was very upset.

Johnny said, "I like Malden and its fresh air, and I do not mind traveling to and from Boston for work."

The North End of Boston still had the smell of molasses on a hot day from the Great Molasses Flood

Disaster that occurred in 1919 at the Purity Distilling Company. A fifty-foot high storage tank containing molasses exploded spreading over two million gallons of syrup throughout the North End causing the death of twenty-one people and injuring a hundred-and-fifty others. Horses caught in the large wave of Molasses were also killed. Buildings close to the tower were pushed off their foundations and destroyed. The incident created a wave of molasses reported to be approximately fifteen feet high, flowing at a rate of thirty-five miles per hour that inundated the neighborhood.

Several blocks experienced waist-deep molasses wounding and killing people, horses, and dogs. Rescuers had problems moving through the syrup to help the victims. Some of the dead were completely covered by the molasses leaving it difficult to recognize them. Cleanup was expensive and extensive. Rescuers stopped searching for victims after four days and cleanup in the area took weeks. Repair and reconstruction continued for a long period of time. Molasses was fermented and used to make rum and ethanol as well as a component for making munitions. The stored molasses in the storage tank was awaiting transfer to a facility in nearby Cambridge.

The disaster occurred several years before Anthony, Theresa and Johnny arrived in Boston, though its effects were still being felt. This was not the reason, however behind Johnny's move.

Johnny still did not tell Anthony his prime reason to live in Malden was to detach from Anthony and

Theresa to keep them safe from the possible visit of the New York City Gang. Johnny said his plans had not changed and that he would travel to and from Boston to work, and eventually partner up with Anthony to go into their own business when they were ready. Theresa agreed with Johnny. She would also like to eventually move to the suburbs. Anthony thought about it and said he understood. Many of their North End neighbors discussed moving north to the suburbs. Anthony was glad Johnny had not changed his mind relative to their eventually starting their own business in Boston.

Chapter Nineteen
Love is in the Air

Joey asked Johnny if he wanted to go to an Italian street festival held in their neighborhood over the weekend. It was a block party with several streets blocked off. In the morning there was a parade with a marching band and people carrying a wooden platform on their shoulders holding a religious statue.

In the evening, the band sat in a temporary band stand and played music for pedestrians to listen to. There were many food vendors selling sausages, peppers, chicken, raw oysters, beer and wine.

Joey and Johnny were enjoying the music when Joey noticed his Uncle Dominic DiGiammerino in the crowd. Joey went to greet him and introduced Dominic to Johnny. Dominic was with his wife and his children. He had three teen-aged sons, one baby boy and a daughter who was approximately eighteen years old. She would not look at Johnny. She had an angelic look on her beautiful face. Her eyes were deep brown and her complexion light. Johnny's heart raced. This was the soulmate for him. He stood still and quiet while Joey and Dominic talked. He felt like a fool because he could not think of anything to say. Before he had the courage to start a conversation with the girl, her father had said goodbye and walked away with his wife and family in tow.

Johnny quickly asked Joey her name and told him how he wanted so much to meet with her. Joey told him she was Dominic's oldest child and that her name was Louise. She was Joey's cousin.

"She did not look at me, and I wanted to talk to her, but I was so nervous I could not speak," Johnny said, wishing he had at least said hello.

"It is good that you did not speak to her then. My uncle Dom is very old-fashioned and protective of his only daughter. You must show respect. If you want to meet with her, you must first ask his permission. Any meeting with her would require a chaperone to be present, but even before that, you would have to meet with Dominic alone and ask his permission to meet with her. He will ask you questions about your family, your intentions, your assets and anything else he wants to know about you. You better think carefully before you go any further with this. In his mind, he will be interviewing you as a prospective son-in-law. It will not be possible to date Louise for a casual relationship. If you're looking to hook up with a woman for temporary pleasure, you do not want to pursue this. I can introduce you to ladies in Boston for pleasure without any commitment."

Johnny let it all sink in. He had no interest in any other women other than Louise.

"I still want to meet with her." The decision was made.

"Remember, Dominic is my uncle. He is family. I would have to introduce you as my trusted friend. Anything you do or say when you meet him will also reflect on me. I want you to think about this. Let's not talk about this for a couple of days and then we will discuss it again."

Johnny was already smitten. "I cannot get her out of my mind"

"What did we agree to do? Let it go for a couple of days."

Johnny never felt like this before. That night in bed he tried not to think about her and would try to think about other things, but his thoughts always drifted back to Louise. The next morning, he could not eat. He did not understand. How was this possible? She did not even look at him. He did not even hear her speak. What if she had no personality and a very deep voice. He was out of control. Joey was right. Don't rush into anything.

Johnny did not talk to Joey about Louise for a couple of days as agreed to. At lunch break Monday at work they both sat down to eat.

Johnny said, "I want you to introduce me to Dominic as a possible suitor. I will not cause you any problems with your uncle or your family."

"It is possible he may say no right away. He met you at the festival. He may not like your looks. Are you prepared for rejection?"

Johnny had not even considered that possibility.

"I am asking you, my friend, to do your best to set up a meeting for me with Dominic. Will you do that for me? I will forever be in your debt."

"Yes, I will ask him but be prepared that he will say no," said Joey. "I don't think he will be impressed when he asks what you do for a living and I tell him you are an apprentice meat cutter."

"I want you to tell him the truth. Please tell him that as soon as I complete my apprenticeship my older brother and I will open our own retail business. If you do a good job and Dominic agrees to meet with me, you will be the first employee we will hire at a better wage than your making now."

Joey smiled. "Don't make promises you cannot keep. I will do it because you are my friend and you have been driving me crazy since you first laid eyes on Louise."

"When do you plan to speak with Dominic?" Johnny asked, anxious to meet with him.

"I will visit him if he is available this coming weekend. I want to talk to him when he has time to sit down and have a serious conversation. Hopefully when nothing else is on his mind."

Chapter Nineteen
Young Courtship

Louise DiGiammerino was born in Italy and was brought to America as an infant by her father Dominic and mother Mary DiGiammerino. They settled in Boston. Her mother Mary died several years after their arrival and her father Dominic remarried several years later. Dominic and his new wife had four sons named Anthony, Patsey, Frank, and David. Since Louise was older than her stepbrothers, it was her job to look after the boys when not in school and help her working stepmother maintain the home, cooking and cleaning. Shortly after the youngest son David was born, Dominic moved the family to Adams Street in Malden.

A sad event happened to the family which Louise never would forget. At that time David was an infant. The other three boys attended school as did Louise. It was arranged that Louise would bring David for child care across the street to a neighbor's home every morning before school. They were a young couple who loved children and they would occasionally babysit for some of the other neighbors. They became close friends with the DiGiammerino family and Dominic agreed to pay them to care for David while Louise went to school. After her school day, Louise would make sure the boys returned home from school. She would then pick up David to join the other boys at home and prepare dinner for the family, before her father and stepmother returned home after work. Her working stepmother wanted Louise to stay home from school and care for David, but Dominic wanted his daughter to be educated. Louise was more of a mother than a stepsister to her brothers. She loved them, and they loved her.

Louise looked forward to picking up David each day after school. He was a very happy and lovable child and she received such pleasure taking care of him.

She came home from school one day and went directly to the house across the street to pick up David. She knocked on the door. There was no response. She knocked again harder and still no response. Perhaps they were in the backyard, so she walked around the house. No one was there. She went around front and knocked hard on the door again. She tried to look in the front window. The shades were drawn but there was an opening on the bottom that caused her to go down on her knees in order look in. The front living room looked empty. There was no furniture. She rushed around the sides and back of the house to try to look in the other windows. She could see the house was empty.

Dominic immediately called the police. They found out the house was rented and none of the neighbors knew that they had left. The couple and young David were never seen again. Dominic's wife blamed Louise for not staying home to take care of the child and causing the family to trust strangers. She felt Louise, as a girl, did not need schooling. She would marry someday and would have enough experience taking care of her stepbrothers to become a good wife and mother. Her stepmother was never formally educated and worked in a factory. She believed education should only be for boys who had to be the prime wage earners. She blamed Dominic for spoiling Louise. The loss of young David would stay on Louise's mind for the rest of her life.

Louise continued her education with the support of her father and against the wishes of her stepmother.

Joey set up an appointment with Dominic on behalf of Johnny. Joey brought his uncle a bottle of homemade wine. After some family small talk. Joey got right to the point.

"Uncle Dom, I came here today to ask your permission for my very close friend Johnny Santoro to come and visit you. I introduced you to him at the festival

Young Johnny and Louise

where he became enchanted with cousin Louise. He would like to meet with you to discuss his honorable intentions with the hope of meeting Louise, with a chaperone present of course, to see if a mutual relationship is possible."

121

Dominic was slow to answer. "Louise is my only daughter and has worked hard all her life taking care of her stepbrothers while their mother worked at the mill. Life was not easy for her and she is very special to me. When and if the time is right to leave the fold, the person she will join with must be also very special. Now you must tell me why this Johnny friend of yours is special enough for my beloved Louise. What does he do for a living? What about his family? I have a lot of questions. Why do you think he is good enough for me to consider him for my Louise?"

Joey told Dominic of Johnny's fantastic journey in great detail as Johnny had told him. He talked about the time Johnny had been kidnapped by the Italian militia when he was a young boy, to his present life in America. The only thing he left out was the New York gang incident.

"Uncle Dom, this man is a survivor with great courage and a drive to be very successful. He would protect and provide for Louise if he successfully courts Louise with your permission."

Dominic's answer came swiftly, "Joey, I will not at this time give him any permission to meet my daughter."

"Because you are my nephew and you have gone to this effort to help your friend, I will give him permission to meet with me so that I can ask him questions eye-to-eye to determine in my mind if he is special enough for my Louise. Ask him to come to my house next Saturday afternoon and I will meet with him."

Joey came back to the apartment and asked Johnny to sit down and to listen carefully.

"Johnny, He will meet with you. I did my best, but you have to understand what you're dealing with. In America, meeting girls, dating, courtship, and even marriage is not the same as it is in parts of Italy. My uncle Dominic still thinks and acts as if he was still in the old country relative to family and customs. Most marriages in Italy where Dominic came from were pre-arranged by the parents. In America if you ask a girl on a date usually it is up to her to say yes or no. There is no chaperone. If you're lucky enough to steal a kiss after the first, second, or third date, that's wonderful. That is not possible in Dominic's world. My mother and father were married in the old country. It was a pre-arranged marriage. They did not kiss until the wedding night. They were not in love. They may have eventually fallen in love after years of marriage. I do not know. You do not know what you're getting yourself into. You still have time to back out now gracefully. Do not let your emotions cloud your judgment. Dominic is looking at this situation as an interview for a prospective husband for Louise, not to permit you to ask her out for a date. Again, I ask you to think this over and sleep on it."

Johnny did sleep on it. That night he had a dream that he had married Louise and it was wonderful. Johnny walked the road of life alone since his journey began. It would be wonderful if he finally had someone to walk with him now. It would be a new start for both of them in a great country with lots of opportunity. He wished he could talk to Louise to see if they were compatible, but Joey said that was not yet possible.

The next morning Johnny spoke with Joey. "I appreciate your concern, but I want to take this a step further. I want you to tell Dominic I would like to meet with him Saturday at his home."

"Ok I will do it. Who knows, he may just shut us down and say no after this meeting."

Johnny went to meet with Dominic on Saturday. He brought a gallon of wine. Dominic greeted him, and they sat, talked, and drank at the kitchen table for hours. None of the other family members were present. Johnny was originally concerned about what he would talk about with Dominic. He found that when Dominic asked him about his kidnapping by the Italian militia he started to reply, and his whole life's story just flowed out of him. Dominic was both intrigued and impressed. He asked many questions. Johnny regretted talking about his nick name Johnny Saint Gold, but he drank too much wine and he realized he had to be careful about what he said to Dominic. They concluded their meeting on good terms and Dominic suggested Johnny come by the very next Saturday.

When Johnny returned to his apartment, Joey could hardly contain himself. "How did it go?" he asked enthusiastically.

"Fine, I think. Dominic seemed very friendly. We were like two friends drinking and talking all alone. No one else was there. He wants me to visit again next Saturday."

"Did you discuss Louise?"

"No. He did not bring her up. It seemed he wanted to know everything about me. When I see him next Saturday, I will bring up Louise's name in our conversation."

"Don't rush it. It looks like he enjoys your company," said Joey with a smile. He liked the direction that things were moving in.

"He should enjoy my company. We drank almost the whole gallon of wine that I brought him."

The next Saturday Johnny went to visit Dominic again. The conversation drifted to Dominic's life in Italy and his journey to America. Johnny showed patience and politely listened to Dominic's story. They drank almost as much wine as their last visit together.

Towards the end of his visit, Johnny was about to ask about Louise when Dominic said, "when you come by next week, I will have Louise sit with us."

"That would be great Mr. DiGiammerino. I look forward to it." Johnny left walking on air. His future just got a lot brighter.

Chapter Twenty
Saved Again by Johnny Saint Gold

The next weekend Johnny went to meet with Dominic and was happy that Louise was sitting at the kitchen table when he arrived. Dominic briefly introduced Johnny to Louise. She looked at Johnny, nodded and said that she was glad to meet him.

Dominic did most of the talking. She was very quiet. After a short while she asked to be excused to go on an errand with her stepmother. When the visit was over Dominic told Johnny if he wanted to take a walk with Louise next Saturday at 2:00 PM, he had his permission. The walk would be chaperoned by a friend of the family of course. Johnny happily agreed.

Johnny anxiously waited for the next Saturday to come. He showed up at the DiGiammerino home promptly at 2:00 PM. An older woman that Johnny had never met greeted him at the door. She asked him to sit down in the living room. After a short while Louise came into the room. She said hello and introduced the woman as Mrs. Bruno, a friend of the family. She said they would walk to Fellsmere Park and Pond, which has a walking path. The tree-studded path led around the pond which had a beautiful water fountain in the center. It provided the residents of Malden with a quiet retreat. It is sometimes referred to as the Malden Reservoir. The park and pond were a short walking distance from the Edgeworth section of Malden.

Johnny and Louise walked side-by-side with Mrs. Bruno following shortly behind them. Johnny tried to get a conversation started by telling Louise about himself, but he received very brief responses from her. He felt she did not like him. Perhaps her father had forced her to walk with him. He thought of what Joey said about arranged marriages. Of course, why would anyone want to be involved with another person if they did not know or like them? They had reached the entrance to the park. It was beautiful. There were lots of trees and grass on one side of the walking path and the pond on the other side. A couple were walking in the same direction about a hundred

Fellsmere Park and Pond, Malden MA

feet in front of them. Johnny felt that this whole thing was a mistake. He did not want a relationship with Louise if she did not like him. He should have known she was not attracted to him. She did not even look at him when he met the DiGiammerino family at the Italian Festival. He decided to ask her questions about her life. Maybe he talked too much about himself. No, this was not working. Her responses were just as brief as before. He could not wait for the walk to be over.

They were about halfway around the pond when he decided that he would take Louise and Mrs. Bruno back to the house and say goodbye. He would tell Joey to talk to Dominic and tell him they were not compatible. No, he did not want Louise to be blamed. He would have to think about what he would say. Johnny turned his head to look at Mrs. Bruno who had dropped back preoccupied with looking at the beautiful pond and a family of ducks crossing her path. She carried a large bag with shoulder straps.

Johnny and Louise continued their walk with no additional conversation with each other. Johnny could not wait for this experience to end.

Two young men, one tall and thin and one short and stocky, walked towards them from the opposite direction and continued to walk by. He looked over to Louise and she looked straight ahead, not noticing that Johnny was looking at her.

They heard a loud scream behind them and turned to see Mrs. Bruno struggling with the two men that had just passed by. They were trying to grab her bag, but she resisted. Johnny ran as fast as he could, but she had dropped back considerably. They saw him running towards them and turned to face him as he moved closer. Johnny ran right into the tall man with both arms and fists alternately swinging. He hit the man hard about the head and face several times and the man went down while trying to cling to Johnny. Johnny went down on top of him.

The short man picked up a rock and hit Johnny in the back of the head while he was down. He was going to hit Johnny again with the rock when Mrs.

Bruno swung her bag and hit the man in the back of his head. Whatever was in the bag was hard enough to knock him away from Johnny as he was getting up to his feet. Blood trickled down Johnny's back from a big gash in the back of his head. The tall man on the ground had trouble getting up. Johnny went after the short man who hit him with the rock.

Johnny hit him several times in his face causing blood to flow profusely from his nose and mouth. The man turned and ran. The tall man on the ground got up and pulled a knife out and slashed Johnny. The knife cut into Johnny's side. Johnny grabbed the hand holding the knife and twisted it until the knife dropped to the ground. Johnny punched him several times knocking him to the ground again. He got up, turned, and ran. Johnny attempted to follow him, but he fell down on one knee and remained motionless for a few seconds. His head ached, and he felt dizzy. The knife cut was not deep but there was blood all over the side of his shirt.

Louise came to Johnny. Her face was as white as a ghost.

She had tears in her eyes. "Johnny, are you okay?

Johnny assured Louise that he was fine. He turned to Mrs. Bruno with an unexpected question. "Do you mind me asking, what did you have in your bag?"

"Two Eggplants I picked up at the market on the way to Louise's house."

They all laughed and hugged each other. Louise grabbed Johnny's hand and they all walked down to the water's edge together. Louise looked at Johnny's knife wound. "It is not deep, but we should go to the hospital to see if you need to have stitches."

Louise's attitude toward Johnny changed right after the encounter with the two men who tried to steal Mrs. Bruno's bag. She had initially been reluctant to be friendly with him. Her father tried to push her into a relationship with someone she did not know or possibly didn't even like. He was handsome enough, but he spoke broken English. She was practically born in America. She was brought over as an infant. She was educated. This was not like her father to welcome a stranger into the family fold just because her father and Johnny had wine drinking sessions together every Saturday. Her stepmother contributed to her father's lack of good judgment in this matter by constantly telling Dominic that it was time for Louise to leave the household and have her own family. But now she was impressed with Johnny's brave actions relative to his defense of Mrs. Bruno. This new relationship deserved a second look.

Dominic was also impressed with Johnny and invited him over to join the family for their traditional Sunday feast. The meal would start promptly at 1:00 PM and last most of the day with serving-after-serving of Italian soup, pasta, meats, and salads, and of course home-made wine. Dominic repeated his invitation each week and Johnny soon became a permanent member of the DiGiammerino family Sunday feast.

Louise grew very fond of Johnny and after a short period of time, they became engaged. In the meantime, Johnny and Joey completed their apprentice program and were transferred to the same department in work as Anthony. Johnny and Anthony had enough money saved to start their own business. They started their search for a good location.

Chapter Twenty-One
An Unexpected Reunion

Anthony found a location for their new business venture. There was a basement rental available on Blackstone Street in Boston that had everything they needed. There was access down to the basement facility from the street by a wide cement stairway with railings on both sides. There was street-level wooden and glass product show stands on each side of the stair railings. The glass enclosed stands could be used in the winter to display various samples of meat cuts with price tags which could be purchased below. The large area below had work benches, scales, chopping blocks, a small partially glass enclosed office, and a huge walk-in freezer.

They signed a lease and put down a deposit. They pooled their money to buy knives, supplies, and product. They asked Joey if he wanted to join them as a partner. He had no savings at the time but said he would like to work with them if they could pay him a reasonable wage. They purchased product and opened for business.

The first day was hectic but very successful. There was constant walking traffic on the sidewalk and the many fruit stands lined up on the street intensified sidewalk traffic by their newly-opened shop. At the end of their first day they had depleted most of their inventory. It was a good location and each day led to increased sales. Anthony sold a very large order to a customer who asked if they would deliver the order to his market in nearby Somerville the next day. Anthony agreed to do so. They did not have a refrigerated vehicle but fortunately the weather was cold, and Joey was able to deliver the order to Somerville. As time passed, they picked up sales from additional small retail stores in the suburbs of Boston which increased their revenue. Joey was put in charge of the delivery part of the business. The business was very successful, and money rolled in. They added an accounting clerk and two more meat cutters and salespeople.

Louise fell in love with Johnny, despite their initial arranged meetings initiated by her father. Johnny was in love with Louise from the first day he met her. They married

Blackstone Street, Boston MA

in The Immaculate Conception Church off The Fellsway in Malden on a Saturday morning. She looked beautiful in her gown and Johnny stood tall and handsome in his tuxedo. Louise's father Dominic arranged a big wedding reception in a large banquet hall in Malden with an orchestra and catered meal. The menu included Italian wedding soup, ravioli, meatballs, sausages, antipasto as well as a very large wedding cake. The guests lined up in a reception line to give Johnny and Louise envelopes filled with cash as wedding gifts. They ate, drank, and danced throughout the evening. It was fortunate for Louise and Johnny that the next day was Sunday. They were both exhausted.

There were many friends in attendance from the market, the North End of Boston, relatives and friends of the DiGiammerino family, and of course Johnny's adopted family, Carmen Pelosi and his two daughters Lucy and Donna. Johnny was happy that his brother Anthony and sister Theresa were there for him. Still, he felt sad that his father and mother were not alive to see how Johnny developed into a successful businessman about to start his own family with his new lovely bride Louise. They did not have a honeymoon since Johnny was required to go to work on Monday morning, the busiest work day of the week. Johnny promised Louise that they would go on a honeymoon sometime in the future, a promise that Johnny was never able to keep.

Johnny and Louise moved into an apartment on Charles Street in Malden, not far from the Fellsmere Park and Pond where Mrs. Bruno was attacked. They were still in the Edgeworth section of Malden several streets from the DiGiammerino household. A year after the wedding Louise was pregnant. She had their first child and named her Mary. One year later She was pregnant again and had a boy named Anthony after Johnny's brother. They nicknamed him Tony.

One morning Johnny and Anthony had to leave the store to see their banker. When they arrived back at the store their clerk told Johnny that two men dropped in looking for Johnny Saint Gold and Anthony Santoro. They left without giving their names and told the clerk not to mention their visit.

They would be back again. They told the clerk they were friends and wanted to surprise Johnny and Anthony.

Johnny froze and knew he had not used or told his nickname to anyone in Massachusetts, except for Joey and his father-in-law Dominic.

Could these visitors possibly be from the gang in New York still trying to avenge Angelo's murder so long ago? Johnny told the clerk not to mention their visit to Anthony. If it was the New York gang, he had to protect Anthony and he had to protect himself. The clerk in the office had a good view of the stairway coming down from the street. Johnny told him to keep his eye on that stairway and notify him as soon as he saw them coming back into the store. He hid boning knifes around the store, even in the walk-in freezer. A boning knife has a thin sharp blade approximately six inches long with a very sharp point. Johnny had been trained to use the knife as part of his trade and it could be a fierce weapon in the hands of a trained meat cutter. He called his foster father Carmen and asked him if he had any visits or inquiry from anyone regarding Johnny. He said he had not.

Johnny remembered that Joey had purchased a small hand gun in the North End and kept it in his apartment in Malden. Johnny asked him if he could help him get a gun to protect Louise and the family at their home.

Joey said, "We could pick one up this coming weekend."

"I want to pick it up now," Johnny said. He was in no mood to take any chances.

"Is anything wrong Johnny? Why the hurry?" asked Joey.

"I promised Louise I would get one a while ago and I forgot and now she is bugging me. Let's go."

Within an hour Johnny and Joey were back at the market with Johnny carrying a loaded hand gun in his pocket. Johnny felt he was ready to confront the visitors if they were from the New York gang.

The next day Johnny carried the handgun in his pocket and waited for the return of the

Turn-of-the-Century Butcher Shop

visitors who were looking for Johnny Saint Gold. He asked his clerk to keep his eye on the stairway again and alert him as soon as the two men enter the shop.

He told the clerk, "If you see them, ask them to wait in the office and come and get me and not to mention any of this to Anthony."

Days passed, and Johnny and Anthony were checking inventory in the freezer at the end of the day. Johnny left Anthony in the freezer and went out to get a ledger from the clerk in the office. As soon as he opened the freezer door, he saw two men coming down the stairway and the clerk approaching them. The shop was busy with his sales staff waiting on customers. The clerk turned and looked toward Johnny and raised his eyebrows towards the two men and led them into the office. It was an awkward moment. The clerk did not leave the office as he was told to. He continued to talk to them. The office walls were clear glass on top, so he could see the two men talking to the clerk. He wanted to confront the men alone. He did not want the clerk, or anyone else, in the office. He did not want anyone else to be hurt if the confrontation did not go well.

Johnny could see the men's faces through the glass partitions. They looked older than Johnny. Both had gray handlebar mustaches and were either dark skinned or spent a lot of time in the sun. Johnny thought they looked familiar and he may have met these two when he and Ray visited Angelo. At that time, he was briefly introduced to several people who worked for Angelo. Yes, these men have finally found him. Hopefully they would ask him questions relative to his relationship with Angelo and he could tell how he owed so much to him. He would tell them Angelo brought him to America and he would never do anything to harm him. Would they allow him to explain or would they have their mind made up that Ray and Johnny were Angelo's executioners? After all, Ray quickly disappeared after Angelo was killed. That alone looked as if Ray was involved.

Johnny's head throbbed. He wore a white apron over his white meat cutters frock and quickly took off the apron throwing it on a work bench. He had the handgun in his right pocket and slid his hand in the pocket and grabbed the gun. Johnny approached the office door opening. The door was left open during the work day and the clerk looked out the doorway and saw Johnny approaching. Johnny motioned with his left hand for the clerk to leave the office.

The clerk noticed that Johnny had a stern look on his face and quickly left the office, stepping through the doorway allowing Johnny to enter the office and face the two men.

"How can I help you?"

"We are looking for Johnny Saint Gold. Is he here?"

Johnny hesitated to answer. They apparently did not know that he was the Johnny they were looking for.

"No, not right now. How can I help you?"

He held the gun tightly in his hand without removing it from his pocket.

"If Johnny is not here, Is there an Anthony Santoro here?'

Before Johnny could reply Anthony poked his head in the door and asked, "What is going on, Johnny?"

"I can take care of this, Anthony."

One of the visitors asked, are you Anthony Santoro?"

"Yes I am."

"We wrote to you and told you we were coming. We are Nick and Frank from Spain, friends of your brother young Johnny Saint Gold."

Johnny's mind was spinning. He took his hand off the gun in his pocket and reached out to them to shake their hands and said, "I'm Johnny!"

They all hugged each other and sat down for a good old reunion discussion in the office. Frank and

Nick could not recognize Johnny due to his transformation from the young boy they knew to this tall and well-built man that stood before them. They kept in touch with Anthony by mail for many years. They wrote Anthony that they had both done well in Spain, both were now married with children, and they had decided to come to America. In their last letter, they told Anthony they were coming to Boston to visit them. Anthony wrote them a reply and informed them where their business was located on Blackstone street in Boston. He did not tell Johnny about their plans to visit when they come to America. He wanted it to be a surprise to Johnny.

Anthony invited Frank and Nick, and Johnny and Louise over his house for a reunion dinner the next day where they ate, drank, and reminisced about the days spent in Africa after the battle of Adwa.

Frank wanted to see New England and move on to settle in New York City. Nick and his family decided to stay in a suburb of Boston. They would all continue to stay in touch with each other for the rest of their lives.

Johnny was happy to see Frank and Nick again and was relieved that they were not from the New York gang. Maybe he could stop worrying about Angelo's death and move on to providing for his growing family. Johnny and Louise both wanted children. Johnny was happy and felt fortunate that the business was successful enough to allow them to do so. Several years passed and Louise delivered a baby girl they named Phyllis, and two years later, a baby boy they named Alfred.

Chapter Twenty-Two
Paid Protection?

A business owner two blocks down dropped in to talk with Johnny and Anthony and asked them if they were approached by anyone representing the so-called Neighborhood Insurance Company. They said they offered business protection for a fee. He said it was apparently a scam and asked them to leave. His shop was robbed that night and all his expensive scales were smashed. They left a note threatening that if he went to the police they would strike again. The note also said they knew where he lived. He said he talked to some of the other business owners in the neighborhood and there were several who were approached and threatened.

Some of the other business owners believed that local mafia was responsible, and although they did not want to pay a protection fee, they were afraid to notify the police. Anthony said he would talk with his in-laws who owned the business that previously employed them and ask what they know about this problem. They would know how to handle the situation. For the moment, Johnny and Anthony would not do anything about it. They were not approached by anyone. In the meantime, they would carry on their business as usual.

Johnny loved candy and would always keep a basket full behind the retail counter to satisfy his sweet tooth and for the children who accompanied the retail customers. Every Monday a tall, thin, well-dressed lady named Rosemarie would come to shop with a young boy named Frankie who wore a brace on one of his legs. If Johnny or Anthony were available to wait on her, they would always lift the basket over the counter to enable the boy to fill his pocket with candy. It was apparent that the woman had means. Her driver would stand behind her to carry the meat order when her shopping was completed. She always purchased the best cuts of meat and never questioned the price. They would look forward to her visit and grew fond of Frankie. The boy enjoyed coming to the shop and always had a big smile when the candy basket was presented to him. This type of customer was one of the reasons that Johnny and Anthony enjoyed coming to work in the morning.

Johnny and Anthony informed the sales staff that if they were not available to wait on Rosemarie when she came in, whoever waited on her should make sure Frankie was allowed to fill his pockets with candy.

Several days later there was a visit from two men representing the Neighborhood Insurance Company. They asked to speak to the proprietors and met with Johnny and Anthony in the office. They mentioned that they offered private around the clock protection for the businesses in the neighborhood against break-ins or robbery. They said the police could not provide protection to prevent break-ins or robberies and only got involved after the damage was done and reported. They on the other hand, would be in the neighborhood around the clock watching over the businesses that they protect. The fee would be minimal and paid in cash once per week. Anthony and Johnny told them they would think about it and would give them an answer in a week or so.

Anthony met with his in-laws the next day and asked for their advice. He was told that there was nothing he could do about it. If he refused to pay and notified the police, he eventually would be robbed, and his equipment would be stolen or damaged. Their advice was if the fee was minimal, to just pay it. Anthony and Johnny were reluctant to pay, but the fee was minimal and most of the other businesses also agreed to pay for phony protection.

The cash was collected every Monday morning before retail customers started their shopping. Business was good and seemed to be going well until the minimal protection fee was no longer minimal. They started to increase the amount of the fee until Johnny and Anthony felt it was more money than the business could afford. At first, they thought of going to the police, but then decided to meet with some of the other businesses who were also paying for protection. No one wanted to rock the boat. They were all convinced that refusing to pay would be very dangerous.

Anthony told Johnny he thought he knew who was in charge and he would go and visit him. He would explain that the amount of the original fee was reasonable, but the increased fee was eating into the profitability of the business. Although Johnny wanted to go with him, Anthony felt it would be better for him to talk one-on-one with that person. Anthony left on a Friday morning to make his case and told Johnny he would return after the meeting. The work day was over, and Anthony did not return.

It was time to close the market. Everyone went home except Johnny, who did not know why Anthony did not return. He was worried all day and now he was in a panic. Anthony would not tell Johnny where he was going or who he was going to meet. Johnny could not even call the police. What could he tell them?

Anthony's wife Anna called Johnny and asked what time Anthony left the market, because he was late for dinner. Johnny told her he was waiting for Anthony to return from a business meeting and he would have Anthony call her as soon as he returned. Johnny called Louise and told her he would be home late. Johnny continued to wait in the office, then decided to walk up the stairway to the street to get some fresh air. He was shocked to see Anthony propped up, sitting alone on the top stair. His face was bright red covered with blood. Both eyes were puffed up with one eye completely closed and the other slightly opened. His jacket was covered with blood. He had been beaten badly, could barely talk, and was in terrific pain.

Johnny was about to help Anthony up when Joey appeared at the top of the stairway returning from making deliveries. He finished late and decided to stop off at work to call his lady friend in Boston. He wanted to stay with her for the night rather than make the drive to Malden.

They both helped Anthony to his feet and moved him to a chair in the office. They washed the blood from his face, removed his bloodied jacket, and gave him a glass of whiskey from a bottle in the desk drawer stored for special occasions. Anthony had pains in his rib cage and they all agreed he was in no condition to go home that night. Anna would be frightened to see him in this condition. Johnny called Anna and told her that when Anthony returned, he slipped on the top step on a piece of meat fat and fell done the stairs.

Johnny convinced Anna that Anthony was fine, but they were heading to Mass General Hospital to check out a bruised rib and Anthony would call her later. Johnny told Anna they were leaving right away and asked her to call Louise and tell her what happened and not to wait up for Johnny. He was planning to stay with Anthony until he was treated and released from the hospital. When they arrived at the hospital, Johnny told Joey to go home since there was no reason for both of them to stay. He did not want Joey around when he asked Anthony who did this to him. Anthony was brought into a treatment room and Johnny sat in the waiting room. Johnny thought he must avenge what happened to his brother. They would not get away with this. He would make them pay. After Anthony was examined and treated, he was released. On the way home Anthony told Johnny what happened.

"Johnny, I went to meet with the man in charge of this so-called business protection insurance. I wanted to reason with him to reduce the amount of weekly cash that we are responsible to pay."

"What is his name and where did you go?" Johnny asked, ready to make a visit to whoever had harmed Anthony.

"I am not going to tell you for your own good. These are bad people and I know you are looking for revenge for what happened to me. We have to decide to either continue to pay them or go to the police. This is a big Mafioso gang and we are no match to take them on. I am tired and hurt and going to take some time off to recover. I want you to continue to pay them while I am gone and then we will decide what we should do when I come back to work. I want you to promise me to pay them and control your temper. Will you do that for me?"

"Yes, if you promise that you will never do anything like this alone without me, ever again."

Several days passed and it was the day that the cash would be paid to the same two men who collected every week. They usually came in early before the retail customers. Johnny carried the envelope with cash in his pocket to give them as he had promised Anthony. That morning they did not show up.

Little Frankie, Rosemarie and her driver came in early to the shop. Frankie was handed the candy basket as always. Frankie took a handful of candy and put it in his pocket and with a broad smile on his face said thank you to Johnny. Rosemarie proceeded to give Johnny her food order. Johnny noticed the two collectors enter the market far to the right of Rosemarie and Frankie. The market had become very busy with retail customers waiting in line.

Johnny was about to excuse himself from assisting Rosemarie to go over and hand the envelope containing the cash to the collectors when suddenly a strange thing happened.

Rosemarie walked over to the two men and said, "What are you two doing here?"

"We shop here," one of them replied almost cynically.

They looked around and called out, "Johnny, we will be back later when you're not so busy."

They turned and left. Johnny was confused and did not understand what had just happened. The collectors usually waited for Johnny or Anthony to be free and step to the back of the counter to get the envelope full of cash in private. Johnny completed Rosemarie's order, they both said thanks to each other and she left.

He heard her as she approached the two men. "Why are you here?" she asked, clearly not pleased to see them. It was quite obvious that she knew them. Why did they leave before they collected the cash? They did say they would be back.

A busy day was soon over. It was closing time and the collectors did not return. Johnny closed the market and went home. He could not sleep that night thinking about what had happened that day. He opened the market the next day and expected the two collectors to drop in early to get their cash envelope. They did not come in as he expected. In fact, they did not return at all that day or any of the following days.

The work week ended, and Johnny met with Anthony that Sunday morning at his home. They both could not understand what was going on. Anthony suggested that Johnny approach the other local business owners that were paying for protection and ask them their current relationship with the two collectors without divulging that the collectors did not pick up the payment during their last visit.

Johnny dropped in on his neighboring businesses the next day and casually asked if any of them had any ideas on how to negotiate lower payments with the collectors. Everyone complained, but no one knew what to do. It was obvious by their conversations that collections were still being made and apparently no one else had been allowed to skip a weekly payment.

The following weeks no one came to collect any money. Rosemarie and little Frankie did not return. Anthony and Johnny felt happy that they had a reprieve from paying for protection although they were sad to lose Rosemarie as a customer.

It was almost a year later that Anthony learned that Rosemarie was the wife, and young Frankie, the son, of the man that was in charge of the protection racket. He was responsible for having Anthony roughed up when he went to visit him a year earlier. Rosemarie must have convinced her husband not to bother Anthony and Johnny for protection money after she met the two collectors in their market.

Rosemarie and young Frankie liked Anthony and Johnny and perhaps she suspected that they would guess her relationship with the mob boss after she confronted the two collectors the last day she shopped there. She never returned to the market again. Fate again shined brightly on Johnny Saint Gold.

Chapter Twenty-Three
In Service

Johnny received a call that his foster father Carmen Pelosi died. Johnny felt bad that he did not visit Carmen often enough after he got married. There was never time to do everything, and he deeply regretted not being with Carmen when he passed away.

Johnny worked hard in the market to provide for his growing family. As the years passed, Louise and Johnny had four more children, Joseph, Teresa, Joanne and Robert, bringing their total to eight children. Louise was forty-two years old when her last child Robert was born in 1938.

Although Louise's first priority was to her eight children and Johnny, she never forgot her young baby stepbrother who had been kidnapped so many years ago. The first years of their marriage, Louise had set aside funds from their budget every week to hire private detectives to find the boy. Johnny knew nothing of this. Her search never resulted in anything positive, but when there were funds available, she continued to hire various private detectives who all said that it was impossible to find out what happened to the boy. The police had given up their investigation years ago.

Anthony eventually sold his partnership to Johnny who continued to work as the sole proprietor of the market. Anthony started out on his own business by building residential houses. Johnny and Anthony built some speculation homes together, but Johnny's primary family income always came from his meat business. There were both lean years and profitable years but there always seemed to be enough income to feed and clothe the family.

Several months after Robert was born, Johnny's and Louise's oldest child Mary was brought into the hospital for a bad sore throat. The doctors said she needed an operation to have her tonsils removed. It was supposed to be a simple procedure. She had the operation and went home to recover but was not well for several months. Her throat was still sore, and she occasionally spit up blood. The doctors said she needed time to get well. Mary, being the oldest child, was a great help to Louise. She helped take care of and loved the other children - especially the new baby Robert who she nicknamed Bobby. Several months later Mary died. Bobby would never see his beloved sister again.

Johnny and Louise were shocked and devastated. They could not get an answer from the doctors about why she died. They were not prepared for this terrible loss. Sons and daughters knew they would eventually lose their parents, but parents were not prepared to lose their children. They could not believe she was gone.

Johnny had lost his mother, father, his foster mother and father, his friend Angelo and now Mary, his firstborn child. The incident put a strain on their marriage and Johnny and Louise barely talked to each other for several months. They would visit her grave often, and often would not talk to each other for the rest of the day.

Johnny never paid any attention to politics or the world news. He worked hard every day to care for his family and did not let World War One or the Great Depression deter his determination to survive in America. After his daughter Mary died, he started to be aware of the news coming from Europe. He would buy the newspaper daily and read what was happening in Italy, Germany, and England. The talk of war disturbed him. His sons Tony, Alfred, and Joseph were coming of age where they could be called into service. As talk of war increased, Johnny could not sleep at night. He hoped America would not get involved.

The two oldest boys joined the Massachusetts National Guard as reservists. At first Johnny was against it, but then he thought they may be safe and never be called to combat duty. The National Guard was not a full-time active army. They would not be called to active duty unless they were needed. Surely the Army would be called first. He did think that the part time military training that they received may help them prepare for the worst. Things moved very fast and England was soon at war with Germany.

Germany declared war against the United States on December 11, 1941 to honor an agreement Germany had with Japan called the Tripartite Pact. Under the Germany/Japan pact, Germany was supposed to come to the aid of Japan if they were attacked by another nation, but not if Japan attacked first. Hitler choose to declare war regardless of the wording of the pact.

The Massachusetts National Guard was activated and Johnny's two oldest sons, Tony and Alfred, were on their way to combat in the pacific campaign. Fortunately, they were in the same company and served together. Although Tony was the oldest of the two boys, Mother Louise asked Alfred to watch over Tony since he feared nothing, never backed down to anyone, and would often get in trouble in school. She thought he may take chances in combat that may be risky. She was not wrong being concerned for Tony's safety.

Alfred was the conservative son. He would always calculate what he would do in each situation. Although he was not as troublesome as Tony in school, he was well built and not one to mess with. Unlike Tony, he did not act spontaneously and would always have control of his emotions and actions.

It was later reported that while in combat in the pacific Islands, Tony refused to jump in the fox holes when Japanese planes attacked the American encampment. The planes would fly low attempting to spray the troops with bullets. Tony would stand up and return fire with his rifle while everyone else took cover. Alfred often tried to physically pull him down into a fox hole when he could. Tony shot and hit a Japanese pilot while flying low, forcing the plane to crash. The kill was witnessed by an officer, but it was not confirmed since the officer was shot and killed the next day before he was able to submit his written report to headquarters.

Meanwhile, Johnny's son Joseph was inducted in the army and was sent to serve in Europe. Joseph was good looking, with a boyish face, slender, always soft-spoken, and friendly. Everyone liked him and worried how he would handle himself when exposed to combat. He was never involved in skirmishes in school like his older brothers.

To everyone's surprise, Joseph was awarded a medal for volunteering to take a truck caravan behind enemy lines to save a group of Army nurses from being captured. Joseph said they were all very grateful to him when they were returned to safety.

Johnny would always invite anyone he met with a military uniform, on leave or discharged due to injury, to his home for dinner. He felt helpless not knowing that his boys were safe and wanted to do what he could for the boys returning. He would ask them where they served and if they ran into his boys, knowing that the chances anyone would know them was highly improbable.

During the war there were air raid blackouts at night. This required everyone to pull down their window shades so light would not be visible outside. Any lighting seen from the sky could aid enemy planes to target the populace. Loud sirens would alert everyone that a blackout was being initiated. Air raid wardens would walk their assigned neighborhoods looking for lighting from houses and would ring doorbells to notify the tenants that they were not in compliance with the blackout rules. They were told to either turn their lights out or pull down their shades. Everyone usually complied when they heard the sirens, since they did not know whether it was a real air raid or an exercise.

One evening a call came through from a military hospital from Johnny's son Tony. He said he would be home soon. He was not physically injured but had been discharged due to malaria. Alfred returned home several months later also afflicted with malaria. They occasionally suffered flu type symptoms. It was many years before they were symptom free.

News came that one of Tony's and Alfred's friends had been killed in combat. This reminded Johnny and Louise that their son Joseph was still in harm's way in Europe. The worry took its toll on both of them and caused Johnny to consume more alcohol than he should. There was no news where Joseph was, or if he was safe. At this time the family lived on the second floor of a two-family house on Emerald Street in Malden, Massachusetts. They worried about receiving a telegram or a visit from the military and would react quickly when the front door bell rang. Several weeks later the war ended, and still no word from Joseph.

One day the doorbell rang, and the Bobby ran downstairs to answer the door. When he unlocked and opened the door there was a soldier with a mustache standing in the doorway. Bobby was too young to remember Joseph when he left to join the Army, but he had seen pictures of him - and this man was not Joseph. Joseph was thin without a mustache.

Louise called down to Bobby and asked him who was at the front door. Bobby yelled back. "Some soldier, not Joseph."

Louise leaned down over the railing and looked at the soldier and said, "How can I help you, are you a friend of one of my boys?"

"It's me Ma, Joey."

Louise screamed and ran down the stairs while Joseph ran up to meet her. They hugged for what seemed like forever. Louise cried, "Oh my God. You gained weight and you have a mustache."

When Johnny came home that night the family celebrated, and Johnny and Louise were relieved that all of their boys had survived. Tony and Alfred went to work at Johnny's market and Joseph went to work at Lewis's candy factory. Tony was the first to announce that soon he would marry Virginia, a girl he was dating. Alfred followed with the same announcement that he would marry a girl named Judy. Things were moving fast in the Santoro family. It wasn't long after that Joseph announced his engagement to his sweetheart Jean.

Chapter Twenty-Four
Beginnings and Endings

Just after the boys returned from the war, Johnny received word from relatives in Italy that Big John his protector, foster guardian, and friend in the military in Africa, had died. Johnny felt the days were going by too swiftly. He realized that nothing on earth was permanent.

Johnny was pleased to have his sons Tony and Alfred work with him in his market to learn the trade. He also needed the help. Joey left to start his own business before the boys came home from the war. Tony stepped in and took over the delivery end of the business. Alfred learned the meat cutting trade from Johnny and soon became head meat cutter and market manager. Johnny did not have the energy he used to have and was able to slow down and reduce his work hours with the boys help. For the next several years Johnny worked shorter hours. He left the responsibility of running the market to his boys. Competition by other new similar businesses in the area started to cut into the sales and earnings of Johnny's market. Over the years the business had been good and provided well for Johnny and his family, but it no longer had the customer base of the past.

Several years later Johnny retired and sold the market, dividing the sales proceeds equally with

Tony and Alfred. This helped both boys financially to start their own businesses.

Johnny's brother Anthony was not well and had been diagnosed as a diabetic. He had an amputation of one leg and was fitted with an artificial limb. He still was very active and would do small construction brickwork, carpentry, and tile jobs for friends and relatives.

Johnny would occasionally help his brother Anthony do some small construction projects. One day he stubbed his right big toe while working with Anthony. The toe developed an open wound which would not heal. Johnny never trusted doctors since he lost his first daughter Mary after she had a tonsillitis operation and died. After constant pressure from everyone in the family, he finally went to the doctor's office. Johnny was also diagnosed with diabetes. He was told the toe would not heal. He waited too long, the toe had to be removed. He was also told that he was drinking too much wine for a diabetic. He agreed to have the toe removed but did not cut back on his wine consumption. He always had a gallon of homemade wine under the kitchen table and would drink more than he should. If he had visitors drop in, he would drink with them and if he was alone, he would always have a glass of wine in his hand.

Louise worked hard all her life to take care of her husband and family. One sad event in her lifetime that she could not forget was the loss of her baby step brother David who was kidnapped. It haunted her.

Her youngest son Bobby and his wife Mary had a baby boy that they named Jimmy and wanted more children. Mary had a hysterectomy after Jimmy's birth and they decided to adopt. There was a very long waiting list for adoptions at the time in the United States. Mary had relatives living in Newfoundland. Her aunt worked for the government and was able to help them adopt a four-year-old boy named David. The boy was blond and handsome. He had lived with his grandparents who were not well, and David was eventually put in an orphanage. David's grandparents apparently spoke French and David spoke baby French. When they picked David up, they stayed in a hotel. They went out for dinner and David had a hearty appetite but could not finish the adult meal they ordered for him. They took his leftovers back to the hotel room and watched little David hide the food under his clothes in the dresser drawer. It was obvious that David was not fed well in the orphanage.

After Louise was introduced to her new grandson, she said she felt somewhat relieved of the sadness of losing her baby step brother. Especially when she found out that David was the forename given at birth to her new adopted grandson. She did not previously tell anyone in the Santoro family about the loss of her stepbrother or ever mention that his name was also David. She lost a baby stepbrother named David and was given a baby grandson named David. Fate had again turned a kind eye on the Santoro family.

Eventually Johnny got an infection in the same foot that he lost his toe. The infection did not heal, and Johnny was told he had to have his right foot amputated. Johnny agreed to have the operation. The family was shocked and concerned. They were hopeful that the worst was over. After recovery of his foot removal, Johnny returned home and used crutches to move around.

Johnny seemed to take his illness and its complications in stride and told his family, "What must be done must be done. You cannot worry about it. Worry has no effect on the future." His attitude was nothing short of remarkable.

Shortly after, Johnny developed a wound which would not heal above the foot that was amputated. The doctors tried to treat the wound but unfortunately it would not heal. Gangrene eventually set in. The doctors recommended another amputation just below the right knee. They wanted to save the knee, so an artificial limb would be easier to use. His sons wanted a second opinion. Johnny stubbornly told them no.

It was obvious to Johnny that the amputation had to be done, and he had gained trust in his doctors.

"When you have a bad tooth and the dentist wants to remove it, you don't ask for a second opinion if you trust the dentist. It is my leg. The wound in my leg will not heal and I trust the doctors."

Johnny & Louise - Later in Life

Johnny returned to the hospital to have his right leg amputated just below the knee. Louise was told that she could visit Johnny in the recovery room and was met by his doctor prior to going in to see Johnny.

"Mrs. Santoro, I wanted to talk to you before going in to see your husband. First of all, the amputation went well. I expect him to be physically fine. Sometimes amputees are traumatized by the loss of a limb and act strangely for a short period of time. Sometimes they need help from a counselor or a psychiatrist and their problem usually only lasts for a short time."

"I don't understand. What is the problem doctor?"

"When Mr. Santoro first recovered from the anesthesia, he asked the nurse if she would bring him the part of the leg that was removed. She told him that would not be possible. He raised a ruckus and insisted that he see the leg. He said he did not want to keep it, but he would like to see how the cut was made. The nurse called me, and I tried to explain to him that this was not the practice of the hospital and it could not be done. He told me that it was his leg and not the hospital's and if we do not show him it, he will never come back to this hospital should he need another amputation. I told him that you were coming in to see him and I will talk to him again after your visit. I think we should have someone from our Psychiatric Department talk with him. He is still mad and very upset."

Louise laughed and then apologized to the doctor.

"Doctor, I am sorry. I am laughing because I know my Johnny. There is nothing wrong with his mind. He is just different from most of the patients you are exposed to. I know my husband and he wants to see the leg because he is a butcher. That is his trade. He wants to see how the cut was made. I will talk to him. He does not need to see a psychiatrist. Maybe I do, because I married him!"

Chapter Twenty-Five
Watch Me Walk

Johnny survived the operation but had lost a lot of weight. He refused to take pain medication and did not complain.

After a long healing process, He was given an artificial limb and attended rehab. It took a while for Johnny to get used to the prosthesis, but he was a fighter and soon walked without the use of a cane. Two years passed, and his doctor told him they were going to order an updated replacement prosthesis for his right leg which would be lighter and work better. He now had two artificial right legs and would joke that if one ever got wet in the rain, he would just change his leg. He also continued to drive a car. He was independent and without fear. There were no complications for several years.

Johnny's youngest son Bobby was closest to Johnny at the time of Johnny's surgeries, since he was the only male child still living at home. The rest of the children, excluding Phyllis, had moved out of the house. They married and had started their own families. Bobby took Johnny to his doctor's appointments and established a very close relationship with his father since his retirement.

Bobby remembered his father working long hours to provide for his family and the many nights Johnny returned home after the children were in bed. Bobby felt fortunate that he was now able to spend time with his father, even if it meant driving to Johnny's medical appointments and waiting together to get in to see the doctors. They would talk for hours about the family and Johnny's past.

Bobby remembered some of the events that he shared with his father while growing up. The family lived across the street from a large park on Emerald Street in Malden at the time. It was late afternoon and Bobby was involved in a fist fight with another boy in the park across the street from their house. The other boy was taller, and with a longer reach, scored more blows than Bobby. His father Johnny came home from work unusually early that day and pulled up in front of their home.

Bobby noticed Johnny getting out of the car and said to the other boy. "It's my father, I've got to go. We will finish another day"

The other boy looked over to Johnny, took off and ran away. Johnny looked at Bobby and waved him over. Bobby ran across the street over to his father who was now on the sidewalk in front of the hedge by the house. He was nervous and was not sure how much of the fight his father has witnessed.

Johnny looked Bobby over. "Come closer to me. Were you fighting?"

"Yes," said Bobby reluctantly. He knew his father would not be happy, but he also knew that he could not lie to him.

Johnny forcedly slapped the side of Bobby's head. Bobby lost his balance and tripped over a hedge.

"Get up and come over here," said Johnny, letting Bobby know that he expected to be listened to. Bobby got back on his feet in front of his father.

Johnny asked. "Were you winning?"

Bobby answered, "No."

Johnny slapped the side of Bobby's head again then turned and went into the house while Bobby followed.

Nothing was ever spoken again of the incident, except for what one of Bobby's brothers later said to Bobby.

"In his own way, Pa was telling you not to fight, but if you do, you better win."

Several years later Johnny cut his finger, and again his injury would not heal because of his diabetes. His doctors tried to treat it, but again they recommended that the finger be amputated. The procedure went well, and Johnny recovered fast as compared to his previous surgeries.

Johnny kept active and continued to help his brother Anthony on small construction projects. The family hoped that Johnny would be finally free from any serious surgical health problems, but as fate would have it, Johnny would need surgery again. He developed an ulcer on the upper part of his left foot. It would not heal.

The doctors said they could operate at his ankle just above the wound as they did on his first leg or operate just below the knee eliminating the possibility of two separate surgeries. They were surprised that Johnny held up as well as he did, considering the pain and trauma that all his amputations had caused. They had told Louise that Johnny was very physically and mentally strong and wished their other surgical patients had the stamina and strong will that Johnny had.

The left leg was removed just below the knee and Johnny gradually recovered. He pushed the doctors for anther artificial limb for the new amputation. The doctors said he had to wait for the stump to heal and that he would need extensive rehab balance training to use two artificial legs. It would not be as easy to learn to walk again as it was with one artificial limb.

Johnny did not want to wait for the new prosthesis. He wanted to walk again and to function as normally as he could. He looked at the spare original prosthesis he had for his right leg and felt he could change the wooden right foot to a left foot.

He spent days designing and reworking the spare prosthesis with the help of a friend who had a cobbler shop within easy walking distance around the corner of their home. Bobby would walk on the sidewalk with the old prosthesis strung over his shoulder and deliver and pick up the artificial leg to and from the cobbler who helped make the changes Johnny wanted.

It was a strange sight. Other strollers would stare at Bobby. One day Bobby found a big paper bag and put the leg in the bag thinking is would look less strange. The bottom of the leg was in the bag, but the top still draped over his shoulder, so he wrapped the leg in a blanket to disguise it completely. It appeared to hide the identity of the leg, but he was stopped by a police control car wanting to investigate what he was carrying in the blanket. Bobby could not wait for the leg to be finished.

The cobbler installed all new leather straps and harness designed to fit his new stump. Johnny chiseled the wooden left foot portion and after it was assembled, they came up with a temporary prosthesis for the left leg. Although it was not pretty, it was very functional. When Johnny put his pant leg down and shoe on, you could not see what it looked like or that it was originally a right leg prosthesis redesigned for his left leg.

Initially, he had to visit the doctor every two weeks to see if the stump was healing correctly. Meanwhile, he asked his boys to assist him with his balance after strapping on his redesigned temporary prosthesis. He practiced walking daily with the two artificial legs. After a short time, he did not need any support and was walking on his own with the use of a cane. Then he walked with no cane at all.

On the days that he had a doctor's visit, he would take off his improvised left leg prosthesis in the car while his son Bobby drove him to the doctor's office. He would walk into the doctor's office using his right leg prosthesis and crutches, so the doctor would not know that he was using his homemade left leg prosthesis at home. The doctor would examine Johnny and he would leave the doctor's office using crutches and the right leg prosthesis. He put on his left leg homemade prosthesis in the car on the way home and would walk out of the car using the two artificial legs leaving the crutches in the car.

The doctor finally agreed to order a new prosthesis for Johnny's left leg. They took measurements and told Johnny that he would have the new device in approximately four weeks. In no time, Johnny was called to come in for a fitting and possible adjustment. A technician put the new device on Johnny while he was sitting in a chair. The new prosthesis fit very well, and Johnny was about to stand when the doctor told him not to.

"Johnny, as I told you before, you will not be able to just stand up and walk. I know you did well with your first prosthesis for your right leg, but you had the use of your own left leg," the doctor said. "Balance was much easier than it will be now with two artificial legs. I want you to learn how to walk again in rehab."

Johnny agreed, but asked the doctor if he could stand up from his chair with the help of the technician who had attached the new prosthesis on his leg. His son Bobby helped as well. The doctor reiterated that it would be difficult for Johnny to initially walk on his own.

Johnny stood up with the technician supporting him on one side and Bobby on the other side. He started to walk several steps when Johnny shook himself free from Bobby and the technician. He continued to walk alone unassisted across the room. Everyone in the room, except for Bobby, was shocked.

Johnny turned to the doctor with a smile and said, "Do you know anyone that can use my crutches?"

They all agreed that they never witnessed anyone adapt to the use of two artificial legs so easily. Johnny and Bobby laughed on the way home from the doctor's office.

Chapter Twenty-Six

The Man on the Bed

Johnny would walk, and eventually drive, with his two artificial legs as if he didn't have a handicap. The doctor asked Johnny if he would mind talking to other patients that were having trouble adjusting emotionally after having an amputation. Johnny agreed to visit them in the hospital following their surgery.

Bobby went with Johnny to visit the first patient with a new amputation. The patient was a sixty-five-year-old man who had his right leg amputated just below the knee. The doctor told Johnny that he would be fitted for an artificial limb after he fully recovered from the operation, but he is very depressed and emotional. Although Johnny walked on his own without the use of his cane, he took the cane with him.

Bobby asked, "Why are you using the cane?"

"To drive home a point," Johnny said.

The man was in a semi-private room in the furthest bed from the door, near a window. It was a beautiful sunny day and he was able to clearly see the Boston landscape from his bed. The doctor introduced Johnny and his son to the patient and explained that Johnny had a similar surgery and asked the patient to talk with Johnny. The doctor left them to talk to the man in the bed closest to the door. Johnny asked the man which leg was removed when suddenly the man broke into tears and could not talk.

Bobby was speechless and noticed that the doctor had turned to look at them from the other bedside.

Bobby silently thought that this was not a good idea.

Johnny quickly responded. "Stop crying!" he said, almost shouting. "You still have your other leg and the new artificial one will make you whole. I cannot feel sorry for you."

Then Johnny wacked first his right leg and then his left leg with the cane and said, "I have two artificial legs and you don't see me cry. I walk and drive and enjoy life every day. Look out that window and see how great it is to be alive and mobile."

Johnny walked quickly across the room and back without the use of the cane as if he was a model. The patient looked at Johnny with his eyes wide open and immediately stopped crying. There was complete silence in the room as if everyone was waiting for someone else to say something.

It was Johnny who broke the silence.

"Push your doctor to order you the new limb. Take control of the situation. Don't sit back and wait for anyone to get you on the road to recovery and walking. Your doctor is a great man, but he has two of his own legs, you don't. Now, I have said what I had to say. If you say anything to me, say it with a smile."

Johnny reached over with his right hand to shake hands. Everyone smiled. A woman had been standing in the doorway silently and witnessed Johnny's visit. She walked over, hugged the patient and turned to

Johnny. She grabbed his hands and said thanks with tears in her eyes.

"You are just what my husband needed."

She looked over to the doctor and thanked him.

The incident was moving. Even though Johnny spoke broken English, his accent helped bring a reality to his presentation. The man subsequently recovered and learned to walk with his new artificial leg. The doctor regularly asked Johnny to call on other patients. Johnny and the doctor developed a friendship that lasted until the doctor retired and moved out of state many years later.

Bobby was impressed with his father. It was hard not to be. The more time he spent as an adult with him, the more respect he had for him. His father Johnny was not an educated man, but Bobby realized that Johnny knew everything in life that was worth knowing, and then some. Bobby eventually became a co-founder and the Executive Vice President of a company that went public. When the first prospectus was printed prior to the public offering of their stock, Bobby gave his father a copy of it to read.

Johnny asked, "Is this the red herring prospectus?"

"How do you know what a red herring prospectus is?" Bobby asked, wondering how his father had ever heard of one, a legal document generated by a private company as part of a public offering of stock.

Johnny replied. "Just because I speak with an accent, don't think I do not know about investing."

Bobby was surprised to learn that his father knew a lot more about sophisticated private placement investments and public stock offerings. Bobby had learned that his father had a deep knowledge of a lot of things he learned over his lifetime without any formal education.

Johnny's brother Anthony continued to struggle with diabetes. He had one leg amputated and was also fitted with an artificial limb. Anthony's wife Anna passed away and the diabetes left Anthony very tired during the day. He would rest every afternoon in his favorite chair with his dog at his side. Johnny and Anthony remained close. One day Johnny received a phone call and was informed that Anthony's house had burned down. Anthony's remains were found in a lounge chair with his dog at his feet. He apparently fell asleep in his favorite chair with his dog next to him and was asphyxiated by the smoke while asleep.

Johnny was not the same after his brother's death. He still drove a car but spent most weekdays with Louise resting watching television. Every Sunday and on holidays, Johnny expected the family to sit down to a feast prepared by Louise and his daughter Phyllis. He would look forward to seeing his sons and daughters and their families gather around the dining room table. An additional portable table was set up for the grandchildren in the living room. After dinner, Johnny would talk about his life as a farm boy in Italy, his kidnapping experience by the Italian militia, the terrible battle he was exposed to, how he escaped from the battle, and how he met Angelo, Frank, and Nick in the desert.

He would tell of his voyage to America, his new adopted family Mr. and Mrs. Pelosi and their two daughters, and all the events that led him to Boston. Johnny continued to visit patients who had lost limbs. On one occasion, Louise received a phone call that Johnny was in an accident with his automobile and was brought to the hospital. He had a heart attack while driving and had hit a tree. No one else had been involved in the accident. When the family arrived at the hospital Johnny was comatose and passed away that evening. He was eighty-six years old when he died. Louise lived to age ninety-six.

So ended the life of a man who's life story defied the odds on so many occasions, a good and honorable man who placed high value on family and friends, a man who lived a life of high honor at every opportunity.

Chapter Twenty-Seven

Epilogue

This is the story of Johnny Saint Gold, the boy from Avellino. He was a good and honest man who had to face some extraordinary experiences during his childhood and throughout his life as an adult. His greatest achievements were to survive his experiences and continue to live life and face the future with a positive attitude. He set an example for all that knew him to be strong and positive. Even after his death, his memory gave confidence and strength to his son Joseph, who also had to succumb to a number of amputations due to diabetes. Joseph eventually lost the use of both of his legs just below his hips and became wheelchair bound for a number of years before he died. As an invalid, Joseph kept busy donating his time producing and managing amateur stage shows for talented children and young adults.

Johnny did not die rich and he did not die poor, but he created a family which had very close bonds, a family that loved him and his wife Louise deeply. In the end, this is the best accomplishment that anyone could hope for.

As a reader of this book, you may ask. "Is this a true story?"

The events you have read about Johnny's life in Italy and when he first came to America were told to me by my father. I have used pseudonyms in this book for some of the people who walked their life's path with Johnny. All the events and characters that are written in this book are exactly as Johnny described.

If you are wondering about the teller of this tale, I am Johnny's youngest son Bobby. I have great memories about my father Johnny, my mother Louise, and my family. These are memories I will cherish always.

The Children of Johnny & Louise

Tony and Virginia married and settled in the neighboring town of Medford, Massachusetts. They never had any children. Tony started his own wholesale meat delivery business to small retail stores. In later life, Tony had a hip operation that was not successful and left him in constant pain. The procedure had to be done again. While he did survive the second operation, shortly afterward he succumbed to colon cancer.

Alfred and Judy married and settled in Malden. Several years passed. Alfred and Judy had a baby daughter named Lois. Alfred went into his own business when his father retired and concentrated on developing portion control meats sold to the airlines and passenger railroad lines. Each piece of meat was cut to be the same size and weight so that each passenger's meal would look exactly alike. He did extremely well financially. Alfred and Judy enjoyed a comfortable life until retirement, when he was required to have open heart surgery. During the operation he had a stroke and was left paralyzed from the midsection down and was on dialysis for his last three years before he died. It was thought that having malaria while in the service had an effect on his kidney failure.

Joseph and Jean married and settled in Malden. He stayed with the candy factory for most of his life until it closed. He then went to work for the Malden Housing Authority. Joseph and Jean had four children: Johnny, Joey, Marianne, and Barbi. Johnny's son Joseph was diagnosed a diabetic and had several amputations before he died.

Phyllis had a boyfriend who died in the war. She never married. She dedicated the rest of her life to her father Johnny and her Mother Louise. She died long after caring for her father and mother.

Teresa married William and had one child they named Billy. She divorced William and married Gene and had three children: Dennis, Robin, and Paul. She lived a long life and died in a nursing home.

Joanne married Michael and had five children named: Mickey, Robby, Michelle, David and Paul. Joanne was diagnosed and died of complications of diabetes.

Johnny's youngest son Bobby married Mary and they had one biological son James and adopted a son David. Bobby lost his wife Mary, who died of a heart attack. He later married Barbara, who had two sons Victor and Nickolas, from her previous marriage. Bobby's adopted son David died of a heart attack at age forty-two.

Made in the USA
Middletown, DE
19 January 2019